CONQUERING
THE BULL AND THE BEAR

TIM NGUYEN

CONQUERING

THE BULL AND THE BEAR

A Holistic Approach to Profiting in the Stock Market

TATE PUBLISHING
AND ENTERPRISES, LLC

Published by Tate Publishing & Enterprises, LLC
127 E. Trade Center Terrace | Mustang, Oklahoma 73064 USA
1.888.361.9473 | www.tatepublishing.com

Tate Publishing is committed to excellence in the publishing industry. The company reflects the philosophy established by the founders, based on Psalm 68:11,
"The Lord gave the word and great was the company of those who published it."

Book design copyright © 2013 by Tate Publishing, LLC. All rights reserved.
Cover design by Rodrigo Adolfo
Interior design by Jomel Pepito

Published in the United States of America

ISBN: 978-1-62295-686-9
1. Business & Economics / Investments & Securities / Stocks
2. Business & Economics / Personal Finance / Investing
13.01.24

I dedicate this book to my wonderful wife, my children, and to all my clients who have given meaning to my life.

FOREWORD

The economic and investment environments in the United States and around the world have changed massively in recent years. These changes include investment media; markets; instantaneous worldwide communication; and governmental actions including fiscal and monetary policy, regulation, and reporting. Institutional investors have produced sophisticated alternative investments to the conventional securities of individual stocks and bonds. In addition to long-established mutual funds that have multiplied over the years, exchange-traded funds are widely available. Complex derivatives have been created that were unknown in the past and still are not understood by many. Therefore, these and other factors necessitate both individuals and institutions to become better informed before making investment plans and actions not only to earn returns commensurate with accepted risk but to preserve capital in changing times.

Tim Nguyen's book provides a worthwhile means for investors to better understand financial markets and to deal with their changes.

These opinions are mine and not those of Arizona State University.

—Jerry B. Poe, Professor Emeritus of Finance
W. P. Carey School of Business
Arizona State University

TABLE OF CONTENTS

Part 3
Understanding Market Behavior

Part 4
Strategy and Discipline

PREFACE

Having gone through the euphoric rise in tech stocks in the late 1990s, the Tech Wreck in early 2000, the real estate bubble in 2007, and finishing with the largest financial collapse since the Great Depression, I have learned that there is no ironclad mathematical algorithm that makes money in financial markets in all conditions. Instead, successful investing is a process and requires a way of thinking that is contrary to how many investors actually think and behave. I will take you through this process and, along the way, help you change the way you think and behave when it comes to making investment decisions. This book combines separate thoughts, research, and concepts by taking a holistic, comprehensive view of the stock market, including where it has been, where it is now, and where it is heading in the future.

Combining multiple disciplines into a cohesive framework allowed me to develop a methodical approach to investing, with the sole purpose of helping investors make better decisions by achieving a level of understanding of the stock market that is as necessary to successful investing as having a map to travel across the country. This book is a summary of how the investment decision making process should be and an attempt to help investors recognize, understand, and change the way they think about investing. The main emphasis of this book is on developing a multidisciplinary synthesis that will aid in the determination of the context in which investment decisions are made and identification of the general direction of the stock market. All stocks are affected by the general trend of the stock market as a whole, thus the determination of the stock market's directional trend or change in trend is the most important tactical decision that investors will make.

INTRODUCTION

Too many investors spend too much time worrying about events that don't make a difference. The key to investment success is to understand your own goals and know when the market is ready to start long protracted moves, either up or down, that are reflective of equilibrium changes in the economy where businesses, consumers, and policy makers have an incentive to change their behavior. In addition, and just as important, investors must know how to differentiate between countertrend moves that are short and less protracted from the ones that are long and deep. Knowing when *not* to do something is every bit as important as actually doing something.

This book will provide a framework for making investment decisions that will stack the odds of success in your favor and help you think differently about how investment decisions are made. This framework is intuitive and starts with understanding your own unique goals, objectives, and constraints. The second step in our framework is understanding the sociopolitical and economic environment. I define *sociopolitical* as the interplay between society and politics in the shaping of overall ideas and priorities of human behavior. Investing in the stock market is a race to figure out what consumers, investors, businesses, policy makers, and financial intermediaries are going to do next and invest in advance of these actions. Part II provides a conceptual framework for assessing the behaviors of key participants in the market insofar as these behaviors may impact the stock market. The third step in our framework seeks to understand how the market, in many of its peculiar ways, may behave in such environments. The final step discusses how you should go about implementing your strategy once you have identified the market's primary trend, which is based on the sociopolitical and economic environment and understanding the market's behavior in that environment. In constructing each stage of this four-stage framework, I've expanded upon some building blocks that are a necessary foundation within each of these stages. This foundation filters the endless sea of investment and market information into a summary of practical and enduring knowledge that can be used in any market condition.

Fundamentally difficult environments that follow systemic financial collapses of the magnitude seen in 2008 require a more complete picture of market behavior and a better understanding of social, political, economic, and credit conditions in order to succeed and overcome the emotional frailties that accompany poor investment decisions. These multiple perspectives are paramount in financial markets when you have a zero-sum game where somebody wins and somebody loses (or at least doesn't gain as much). During my career, I've fielded thousands of thought-provoking questions from investors and have helped many people understand how to make money in financial markets. Throughout this book there are question-and-answer sessions that are based on these conversations, which will serve to illuminate the concepts discussed.

I want to make one thing clear at the outset of this book—there is no algorithmic formula or system that will make you an automatic winner at investing in the stock market. If you are willing to put in the time, discipline, and dedication to learning and understanding the market, this book is an indispensable tool to help guide you in the right direction and stack the odds of success in your favor

With the help of this book and dedicated practice, you will begin to think in different ways and have a framework for making investment decisions that will help you position yourself for lifelong success in investing. With the writing of this book, I have done my part. Good luck!

THE FRAMEWORK

Strategy and
Discipline

Understanding
your goals and
objectives

Understanding
market
behavior

Understanding
the current
macro
environment

Part 1:
Planning Your Investments: Understanding Your Goals—the Path to a Strategic Asset Allocation

Strategy and
Discipline

**Understanding
your goals and
objectives**

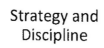

Understanding
the current
macro
environment

Understanding
market behavior

Chapter 1

THE IMPORTANCE OF PLANNING

Part I of this book discusses the methodology, purpose, and concepts behind *planning your investments, which is the most important part of the investment and wealth-planning process because it provides the context in which all other key decisions are made.* The most important reason for the planning phase of the investment management process is that it gives you the confidence necessary to succeed in managing your investments as it helps to reduce the level of emotion associated with the investment decision making process. Any athletic coach in competitive sports will tell you that it is impossible to win without having a game plan. A game plan sets the tone for all other decisions that are made in the game. Failure to plan is planning to fail.

I am amazed by how often I meet potential clients who have amassed wealth well into the millions of dollars but have not done any investment or wealth planning. I remember having lunch with a prospect whose net worth was well over $10 million comprised mainly of land investments, and during the course of our conversation, I asked him if he had done any financial or investment planning given that he was in his midseventies and potentially going to be encountering a liquidity event. A liquidity event occurs when you are about ready to receive a large infusion of cash from the sale of a business or other asset of significant value. He said that he had not done so because he was untrusting of advisors. It took me a few minutes to realize that he was not kidding. Later that year, I met with a different prospect that had $1.5 million in money market funds, which were part of her family inheritance. Living off this money, scared of the stock market and skeptical about advisors in general, she kept her money in money market for over four years (and counting) earning essentially 0 percent! Although these are only two examples, situations like these abound. Even if you have done some investment or financial planning and you have a diversified portfolio, how do you know if your portfolio is truly in line with your goals and risk tolerance given that the investment climate is going to be completely different over the next twenty years than it was the last twenty years? *Whether it be a result of procrastination or skepticism about the process, one should not allow chance to direct their financial future.*

Goals and Objectives

The best place to start in planning what you are going to do with your wealth is to start with your goals and objectives. Some important questions to ask during this phase are:

- Do you need income? If so, how much?
- How frequently do you need this income?
- Do you have special needs children or family members?
- What financial obligations do you have?
- Are you subject to estate tax?
- Do you have philanthropic goals?
- How long do you need this money to last?
- What are your monthly expenses?
- Are you a high-profile person that is sensitive to potentially frivolous lawsuits?
- What other sources of income do you have?
- How reliable is your income?
- How much liquidity do you need?

Answers to these questions will provide the cornerstone for all other wealth decisions that you will make. You may ask, how does this relate to managing investments and making money? Addressing these questions will provide the context in which all other investment decisions are made. Otherwise, how would you know if you are making the right investment decisions if you have no context in which you are making those decisions? *How* you make money is just as important as making money itself because part of the investment management process is managing risk. *Without the proper context, one may fall into the trap of systematically making high-risk decisions that eventually will lead to that one fatal financial mistake.*

Wealth Structuring

Wealth structuring is the process of organizing and establishing the entities to facilitate growing your wealth, protecting your wealth, transferring your wealth, and creating a philanthropic legacy. Many of the topics of wealth planning are also covered by other professional advisors such as estate planning attorneys and tax accountants. A well-planned wealth strategy usually involves careful coordination of your investment manager, estate attorney, and certified public accountant (CPA). What I cover in this section only scratches the surface of all the details and depth of knowledge required to craft a comprehensive wealth plan. The purpose of this section is *not* to find answers and solutions to your broader wealth planning concerns. There are literally volumes of books on these topics and many financial advisors and other professionals that will need to help you. The sole purpose of my coverage of the wealth planning process is to help illustrate the context in which all investment decisions are made and how going through the process gives you peace of mind, which is an important component in helping you take the emotion out of the investment decision-making process.

Growing Your Wealth

Growing your wealth starts with a disciplined savings strategy and locating the tax-advantaged vehicles that are most appropriate. Some tax-advantaged vehicles include:

- Traditional individual retirement accounts (IRAs)
- Roth IRAs
- 401(k)'s
- Employee stock option plans (ESOP)
- 529 plans for college savings

In addition, a large part of a family's wealth may be concentrated in real estate, a family business, or other after-tax savings.

Protecting Your Wealth

Protecting your wealth includes reducing the risk of loss that may result from adverse market conditions through careful risk management and asset-protection strategies that help shield your assets from creditors. Once you reach retirement years, no matter how you define those years, you will want to place heavy emphasis on reducing the risk embedded in the assets that underlie your net worth. This includes reducing the level of concentration that may exist in any one asset. This one asset can be a family business, an individual stock, or a piece of real estate. Reducing the risk of loss due to adverse market conditions is best done through a carefully crafted diversification strategy.

Protecting your wealth by shielding it from potential creditors is a very complex topic best handled by a qualified planning attorney. However, I will plant the seed with some common forms of asset-protection strategies. Protecting your assets from potential creditors typically involves distancing yourself from the control or flexibility of enjoying those assets. Some common asset-protection tools include the strategic use of one or more of the following:

- Family-limited partnerships
- Limited liability companies
- Irrevocable trusts
- Limited partnerships
- Insurance policies

Transferring Your Wealth

The last thing any parent with wealth would want is to die and have no asset-distribution plan. In general, if you are married, the unlimited spousal exemption allows all assets owned by you to pass to your spouse free of estate tax. But this provision is no reason for married couples not to engage in estate planning. If you have young children, who would care for them if you both died? If you have a special-needs family member, how would they be taken care of? Who would get your hard-earned assets? What kind of family feuds would result if you left no direction as to who would get what? There are generally three types of planning tools—contract, wills, and trust.

Contracts are binding and involve designating a "beneficiary." This beneficiary or beneficiaries will receive the assets in the account upon your death. Some examples of contracts include:

- IRA accounts
- Annuities
- Joint tenants with rights of survivorship
- Individual transfer on death accounts

No directive other than a beneficiary designation is necessary to distribute these assets.

Regardless of whether you already have a trust or other estate plan in place, it is still important to have a will. A will designates who is to take care of your minor children if you die. In addition, a will helps to distribute any asset that is does not pass by contract or directed by a trust document. Personal belongings, such as jewelry and memorabilia, would be things that you would want to pass by will.

A trust is a common vehicle used to distribute assets to your heirs. A trust is the legal transfer of assets to a trustee for the benefit of yourself or other beneficiaries. As the grantor of the trust, you have the right to specify how you want your assets to be managed. A trust can be a carefully controlled vehicle, designed to address your specific goals and objectives.

A carefully crafted estate plan that includes a combination of trusts, a will, and contracts will address the myriad of conflicting objectives, which may include:

- Estate tax reduction
- Flexibility with the use of assets
- Control of assets
- Dynasty planning
- Charitable endeavors

Leaving a Philanthropic Legacy

Leaving a legacy involves creating financial structures that will benefit current and future charitable causes. One of my favorite aspects of leaving a legacy is that it helps children and grandchildren understand the importance of philanthropy and instills these values through the strategic use of structures that can facilitate family discussions regarding philanthropic giving. Leaving assets to charities can be done while you are alive or when you die. Typically, income tax deductions are allowed when you transfer assets to a charitable structure or directly to charity while you are alive. Some examples of charitable structures include:

- Charitable remainder trusts
- Charitable lead trusts
- Donor-advised funds
- Family foundation
- Charitable gift annuities

Wealth Planning Summary

Growing your assets, protecting your assets, transferring your assets, and creating a legacy are complex topics that typically balance the following competing objectives:

- Reducing estate taxes
- Maintaining control of your assets
- Having the flexibility to enjoy the use of your assets in any way you define
- Current income tax deductions
- Philanthropic goals
- Asset protection
- Income generation

With regard to wealth planning—and balancing the aforementioned objectives—every family is different and therefore typically requires customization.

Net Worth Composition—the Importance of Financial Assets

Before we can get too deep into managing investments, I think it is important for investors to conceptualize how financial assets such as stocks and bonds fit into their overall net-worth composition.

Whether you classify your net worth composition in terms of asset type (i.e., real estate or financial asset) or objective (growth, income, or safety) the *four most important planning considerations are cash flow, liquidity, growth, and risk management.* In this context, I define *liquidity* as the immediacy of turning an asset into cash. How you compose your net worth will play a large part in the joy or headache of dealing with future financial decisions. I had a client who came to me at the end of 2010 because his advisor had moved out of state. After further analysis of his current portfolio, this client had half of his portfolio in illiquid real estate LLC investments. There were three violations here: one was too much concentration (at the worst possible time), two there was no liquidity for these LLCs, and three there was little income spun off from these LLCs. To make matters worse, he had aggressive income demands and no other source of liquidity or income. I guess his former advisor could not have moved out of state soon enough! I recently had come into contact with a guy who had been a successful real estate investor for the majority of his adult life. The only problem was he did not unload enough of it when the market was high, thus leaving the majority of his net worth in real estate. When I brought up my concern about his liquidity, he said he had it covered by having an equity line of credit tied to the real estate. I would hate to depend on the generosity of a bank for liquid funds if I needed it. When talking to a different real estate investor who viewed stocks as somehow an inferior investment, I asked him why he liked real estate so much. He replied, "At least I can see and kick the dirt" (I guess you can't see and kick stocks). I say happy kicking. Unfortunately, there are many trade-offs between cash flow, liquidity, growth, and risk management. For example, what may grow may not be liquid or income generating, what may be income generating may not grow or may not be liquid, what may manage risk may not grow. Composing your wealth in such a way that best balances these four trade-offs is central to successful investment management.

Financial assets are the most flexible. They are liquid and can be income generating by buying dividends and interest-generating investments. Moreover, financial assets can be structured conservatively or aggressively depending on the objectives of the investor. If you have traditionally only been involved with investing in businesses or real estate, a diversified portfolio of financial assets makes a lot of sense as an asset category because you can achieve liquidity (defined as being able to convert to cash) and have the potential for long-term growth.

Now that I have made a strong argument for the value of financial assets and a conceptualization of how they fit in to one's net worth composition, I will discuss the process of composing your wealth so that it maximizes your chances for future success.

Chapter 2

PORTFOLIO IMMUNIZATION

Portfolio immunization simply means protecting your lifestyle and ensuring that you do not outlive your money. This means preparing for market volatility, potential market catastrophes, general inflation, taxes, etc. A quick and easy way to calculate how much you will need to live the lifestyle you want is to use a divisor that, when divided into the annual gross income need, will result in a target dollar portfolio amount. Harold Evensky and Deena Katz (2006, 223) have called this divisor the "safemax" initial withdrawal rate. The safemax is the withdrawal amount that occurs in year 1. Each subsequent year's dollar withdrawal amount is then adjusted upward by the prior year's consumer price index. For extremely long-lived clients, whom Evensky and Katz call "Methuselah clients," the safemax approaches an asymptotic value estimated to be 3.5 percent, which represents the initial withdrawal rate with which a client could be reasonably confident that his portfolio would, indeed, last forever. For example, let's say you have a gross income need of $150,000 and you have no other income to offset this. With an initial safemax withdrawal rate of 3.5 percent then you would need a portfolio value of $4,285,714 ($150,000/.035) in year 1. In Evensky and Katz's research, they assume that the $4,285,714 portfolio is invested in a balanced 63 percent stock and 37 percent bond portfolio. Let's assume in year 2 that the prior year's consumer price index was 3 percent. In this case, the second year gross withdrawal amount will be $154,500 ($150,000 × 1.03). Let's assume in year 3 that the prior year's consumer price index was 2.5 percent. In this case, the third year gross withdrawal amount will be $158,362. This process continues each year.

I recommend that the portfolio that corresponds to the "immunized" target value be invested *in liquid financial assets*. A financial asset portfolio that consists of stocks, bonds, and commodities can be cash flow generating through dividends and interest and can be liquidated on a moment's notice in case of emergencies. Because liquid financial assets are immediately cash flow generating *and* liquid is a big benefit that is not shared by other asset classes.

Okay, now you may be thinking that a portfolio of $4.2 million is a high hurdle amount to generate a gross income of $150,000 per year. Keep in mind that this target portfolio value, according to Evensky and Katz, ensures that there is *no* chance of outliving one's nest egg given a balanced 63 percent stock and 37 percent bond portfolio. In many cases, people will use a higher safemax rate that reduces the target portfolio value but adds more uncertainty to the longevity of that portfolio. Some common initial safemax withdrawal rates are 4 percent, 5 percent, and 6 percent. The higher the safemax withdrawal rate, the higher the rate of return required by the investor. Using the same $150,000 gross income need would require a target portfolio value of $3,750,000; $3,000,000; and $2,500,000 respectively. Another way to extend the longevity of a target portfolio value other than changing the safemax rate is through active management of these assets and adjusting income depending on market conditions.

The process of retirement income is complicated by the fact that most people have taxable accounts where dividends and interest are taxed and individual retirement accounts (IRA) where the actual withdrawal amount is taxed (with the exception of Roth

IRAs), but the earnings are tax deferred. A detailed discussion on the mechanics of withdrawals from taxable and IRA accounts is outside scope of this book. But I have used *gross* income (before taxes) in my examples to help mitigate the differences between withdrawals from the two types of accounts.

If you have a net worth greater than the amount required to immunize your portfolio, you are now in a position to decide how to invest the rest of the assets. Assuming there is no other objective besides immunizing lifestyle, you are free to invest the excess assets as aggressively and as illiquid as desired. If there is significant net worth and no thought has been given to lifestyle immunization or balancing the competing goals of cash flow, liquidity, growth, and risk management, then perhaps you should start thinking about how to best structure the *composition* of your net worth.

Portfolio Optimization— the Strategic Asset Allocation

The concept behind safemax rate is great for people who have the level of wealth that is high enough that they can carve out a target financial portfolio based on their desired gross income level and a safemax rate of 3.5 percent and essentially have zero chance of outliving their money. But in reality, most people take some degree of risk of outliving their money even if it is a minimal 5 percent or 10 percent chance. In these instances, it is helpful to "back" into a target return. For example, say you want a $75,000 *net* income and you are in the 20 percent effective tax rate. Your gross income need is $93,750. Let's also assume you have a portfolio of $2,000,000. Before adjusting for inflation, you will need a return in year 1 of 4.7 percent. In addition, let's assume that inflation is 2.5 percent per year. Your required rate of return becomes 7.2 percent.

Now, the question becomes, how do you get a 7.2 percent annual return with the least amount of risk possible? The answer to this question is the heart of strategic asset allocation and portfolio optimization. The process is quite complicated and outside the scope of this book; however, I will provide a simplified "user-friendly" version. You take all the asset classes of liquid financial assets, and you estimate what the average annual return will be for each over the next several years. You take the lowest return asset class and place it on one end of a continuum, and you take the best performing asset class and place it on the other end. Once this is done, you pick various points in between these returns. For example:

Stable	Conservative	Moderately conservative	Moderate	Moderately aggressive
Treasury Bills				
2%	4.50%	5.50%	6.50%	7.50%

table 2.1

Once you have estimated the returns as indicated in table 2.1, then the next question is, how do you achieve each of these returns with the least amount of risk possible? To arrive at these answers, you need to know the standard deviation of each asset class and the correlation of each asset class to each other. And using some nice mathematical formula, you solve for the *weights* that go into each of the asset classes for each of the "model" portfolios indicated above. In reality, a computer will do this task. A sample strategic asset allocation for each return requirement listed above could look like the following:

	Stable	Conservative
Return	**2%**	**4.50%**
Stocks	**0%**	**20%**
Domestic large cap	*0%*	*15%*
Domestic mid cap	*0%*	
Domestic small cap	*0%*	
International	*0%*	*5%*
Bonds	**70%**	**73%**
Short	*60%*	*25%*
Intermediate	*10%*	*15%*
Long	*0%*	*25%*
High yield	*0%*	*8%*
Commodities	**0%**	**3%**
Cash	**30%**	**4%**

Given our earlier example that required a 7.2 percent return and looking at the returns for the various optimized (lowest risk for a given return) portfolios, one can conclude that a moderately aggressive portfolio allocation is the ideal risk-return profile.

Conclusion

The process of identifying goals, priorities, and constraints is important because it sets the stage for what legal, business, and charitable structures will help you best accomplish your mix of objectives. Once there is a financial structure in place, you are now in a position to begin investing your assets. When investing money, pay attention to the composition of your investments. When choosing between investing more in a family business, real estate, stocks, bonds, or any other asset, you will want to balance the need for income, liquidity, growth, and risk management. As you progress through the investor life cycle, the balance of these needs change. Therefore, the investment strategy will change in response. Identifying the broader context in which investments are being managed is crucial because it provides a road map of *how* you should go about investing your hard-earned money and assets. The idea is to accomplish your objectives with the least amount of risk possible or maximize return for a given level of risk.

Now that I have taken you through the necessary process of wealth planning, we are now primed to begin investing money. A big part of investing or performing any kind of business is understanding the context in which investment and business decisions are made. Part 2 of this book takes you through the process of analyzing sociopolitical and economic conditions and provides a framework for understanding how to evaluate change.

Question and answer

Question: I have literally dozens of binders in my study that consist of estate planning and other legal documents. Can you help me make sense of these documents so I can begin to grow my assets? I've done a lot of "financial planning" with my attorney but feel more confused now than ever about my longer-term financial security.

Answer: Mr. Smith, let me make sure I understand your asset protection and estate plan. You have:

- A revocable trust with $4.3 million worth of assets
- An irrevocable trust (legally owned by your children) with $8.7 million worth of assets
- A 401k valued at $1 million
- 3 LLCs that are owned by the two trusts mentioned above
- LLC #1 owns your home worth $1 million, LLC #2 owns your rental property worth $2.5 million and $500k of cash, LLC#3 owns your complicated real estate structures and partnerships valued at $6 million and roughly $3 million worth of liquid financial assets
- The revocable trust owns 100 percent of the LLC that owns your home, 95 percent of the LLC that owns your rental property and $500k cash, and 5 percent of the third LLC that has your collection of non–cash flow generating real estate and $3 million in liquid financial assets. The total value owned by the revocable trust is $4.3 million
- The irrevocable trust that consists of assets that you gifted to your children owns the rest. The value of this trust is $8.7 million
- You are fifty years old and looking to retire in five years
- Your objective when you retire is $500k in gross annual income

Mr. Smith, I see a few things wrong here. Before I can help you establish an appropriate investment plan, we need to address the following:

- First, you gifted your own retirement away to your children into their irrevocable trust. I understand that asset values have dropped and therefore it made sense to take these assets out of your estate, but I think you allowed your attorney to talk you into setting your children up for early retirement at the expense of your retirement.
- Second, you have the income rights to your children's irrevocable trust, but the majority of the assets in this trust are non–cash flow generating commercial real estate.
- Lastly, because you have too much real estate, you have very little liquidity given your objectives and the lifestyle you have become accustomed. Your house is not liquid and your rental properties (owned by one of the LLCs, which is in turn 95 percent owned by the revocable trust) are not liquid. What happens if you have a real financial emergency and need to get your hands on a large sum of cash? Or what happens if your tenants run out on you and you no longer have cash flow from your rentals?

Given your current situation, here is the strategy I suggest:

- Get the trustee of the irrevocable trust to unwind out of the non–cash flow generating commercial real estate in LLC #3 as soon as asset values are reasonable and a willing buyer can be found.
- To the fullest extent possible and given the laws of prudence that govern trust law, invest the irrevocable trust as conservatively as possible with a preference toward income-generating assets.

- Invest your 401k moderately aggressive and let it grow tax-deferred for as long as possible.
- Add flexibility and liquidity to the assets that you control directly by selling off some of your rental real estate in LLC #2 (the LLC that is 95 percent owned by the revocable trust).
- Invest the liquid financial assets in LLC #2 moderately conservative
- No more gifting
- Max-out your 401k

If you follow this plan, you will increase your retirement income significantly, add liquidity and flexibility, and add context to your overall investment strategy. Can you see how providing context to your overall situation helps in the management of your assets?

Part 2:
Understanding the Current
Macro Environment

Strategy and
Discipline

Understanding
your goals and
objectives

Understanding
market behavior

**Understanding
the current
macro
environment**

Chapter 3

THE PROBLEM

Now, more than ever, investors need a practical guide on how to make better investment decisions. Global rebalancing is underway with the dominant economic powers making the slow hand off of the baton to the once-peripheral emerging countries. In its simplest form, rebalancing means this: a reset of the global economy shifting the balance of accounts between the world's established and emerging powers or between its biggest consumers and biggest savers. That alone, of course, is a transition of landmark historic significance. Yet it is far from the only consequence, for rebalancing is not just an economic story, but one that will result in a seismic shift in international balance of power in every region of the world.[1]

The market has many players such as hedge funds, sovereign wealth funds, individual day traders, mutual funds, institutional traders, pension funds, institutional investors, and retail investors. Each of these investor groups have different philosophies, approaches, and access to information. In addition, each investor group has its own motivations and constituents. Pension funds and sovereign wealth funds act as a "fiduciary" for their constituents. Institutional traders and hedge funds are motivated by absolute returns. Mutual funds are motivated by relative returns. With so many participants each pursuing their own self-interest and only so much wealth to go around, retail investors as a group are at the biggest disadvantage. Being brutally honest, Charles Ellis, former manager of the Yale Endowment Fund, said: "Investing is a rough and tumble business. It does not matter where these traders work—they may be prop desks, mutual funds, hedge funds, or high-frequency trading shops—they employ an array of professional staff and technological tools to give themselves a significant edge. With billions at risk, they will deploy *anything* that gives them even a slight advantage."[2] The disadvantage faced by retail investors exists because of significant information and knowledge asymmetries and a predisposition toward detrimental emotions of fear and greed. Even within the investment advisory industry, significant gaps exist between information and knowledge. *Many professionals mistake being informed for being knowledgeable. Information turns into knowledge only when you can use that information for profit-making purposes.* The focus of this book is to bridge these asymmetries and provide investors with a greater degree of confidence in making investment decisions.

The disadvantage faced by retail investors is nothing new, but when stock market gains exceed 1,500 percent on a cumulative basis as they did between 1981 to 2000 where everybody was making money (some more than others), nobody cares if you are only making 10 percent per year while other investor groups are making 20 percent plus gains per year. However, problems exist when returns are much harder to come by. The first decade of the twenty-first century resulted in an average annual return of -.51 percent for all stocks on the New York Stock Exchange according to the Yale Center for International Finance. Although I do not expect these dismal returns to repeat in the following decades, one thing is certain, the market has changed. Since retail investors as a group comprise a large part of the market, there is certainly enough money here for other investor groups to gain at their expense. Armed only with a PC, an Internet connection, and CNBC muted in the background, individual investors face daunting odds. They are at a tactical disadvantage, outmanned, and outgunned.[3] As such, it is important for investors to arm themselves with practical insights into market behavior and its connection to the current macro environment to have any chance at success. The objective of reading this book is to provide you with a much clearer understanding of market dynamics, the sociopolitical and economic stage, and a systemic rewiring of how you make investment decisions.

If you were born before 1930 (making you over age eighty as of 2011), chances are you were in your prime investing years *and* prime retirement years during the greatest primary bull market. Consider yourself lucky. If you were born between 1930 and 1940 (making you between age seventy and eighty as of 2011), you are probably glad that your first decade of retirement resulted in very good investment returns and hopefully you did not get greedy. If you were born between 1940 and 1950 (making you between age sixty and seventy as of 2011) you are likely in retirement or preparing for retirement and more concerned than the average investor about the future state of the market. If you were born after 1951 (making you under the age of sixty as of 2011), you have likely accepted the volatility of the market and have given up any hope on the system as a form of checks and balances. Regardless of where you are in the investor life cycle, you will find an appreciation of this book's interdisciplinary perspective on how to profit in financial assets.

The Environment Is Different

The 1981 through 2000, expansive and protracted *primary* ("primary" to be defined in chapter 13) bull market was characterized by the following:

- Deregulation of the savings and thrift industry through the Depository Institutions Deregulation and Monetary Control Act of 1980 and the Garn-St. Germain Depository Institutions Act of 1982 which eliminated the interest rate ceiling that could be charged on deposits. These acts encouraged risk taking at a much needed time.

- The massive productivity that resulted from the personal computer in the 1980s
- The massive productivity that resulted from the Internet in the 1990s
- The growth in high yield bonds popularized by Michael Milken
- A fall in interest rates from 18 percent to 5 percent

Money supply growth over this nineteen-year time frame was the most rapid since 1919. A return to the glory days is unlikely any time soon. The financial collapse of 2008 was the worst and most protracted financial calamity since the Great Depression. The Dow Jones Industrial Average (DJIA), an index of thirty large capitalization U.S. stocks, did not return to its nominal 1929 high until twenty-five years later in 1954. What if the aftermath of the financial collapse of 2008 looks something like it did after the Great Depression?

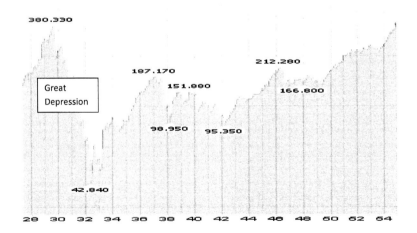

Source: Stockcharts.com

If we had to relive a market similar to what had occurred after the Great Depression, investors would have experienced three significant primary bear markets that resulted in drops of 47 percent, 37 percent, and 22 percent and spanned seven of the twenty-one years following the bottom in 1932. Even investors with a more balanced portfolio would have experienced a great deal of anxiety and frustration with this level of volatility; a retired investor would have experienced a great deal worse. Although investing for the "long term" is important, and the long-term trajectory is positively sloped, *what is more important is investing for the time frame that is unique and important to you.* Being told to think long term while you are being whipsawed by the market during a time that is most paramount is no consolation.

Forget about the 1932 to 1954 period, what if the next sixteen years closely resembled the market from 1966 to 1982?

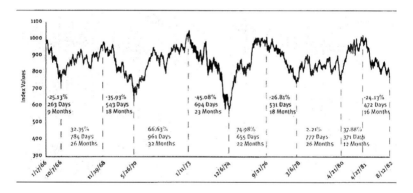

Source: Rydex Funds

During this sixteen-year time frame, investors experienced four significant primary bear markets with declines of 36 percent, 45 percent, 27 percent, and 24 percent that spanned seven of the sixteen years. Investors would have spent almost half this period in a protracted and long primary bear market.

The decades following the Great Depression were characterized by heavy regulation. In 1933, Congress passed the Emergency Banking Bill, Glass-Steagall Act, the Farm Credit Act, National Industrial Recovery Act, and the Truth in Securities Act. In 1934, Congress formed the Securities and Exchange Commission and Federal Communications Commission to help regulate these acts. The late 1960s and 1970s were characterized by stagflation. Stagflation occurs when you have inflation but no growth. The 1970s were characterized by the only peace time period where inflation consistently exceeded 5 percent while unemployment increased by 30 percent relative to the average unemployment rate during the 1960s. Although one must be very careful in extrapolating historical market performance into the future given a similar set of sociopolitical and economic conditions, I believe that market prices and their accompanying volatility do reflect social anxiety associated with whatever conditions are present at that time. Social anxiety created by a slow economy and political jawboning will create a lot of volatility in the years to come.

Similar to what occurred after the Great Depression, the period following the financial collapse of 2008 can be characterized by a heavy dose of regulation. The Dodd-Frank legislation that was enacted in 2011 consists of over a thousand pages aimed at providing better supervision and compliance of financial institutions. This piece of legislation is arguably the most important since Glass-Steagall in 1933, which separated investment from commercial banking. What usually happens when there is a heightened regulatory environment is business and state interests clash.

I do not believe we will see a seventies-style stagflationary environment because the record stimulus following the 2008 financial collapse should create growth and a commodity supply shock, which characterized the 1970s, is unlikely. Regardless of the terms used to describe a period that follows a financial collapse, recession, and asset bubble all occurring at the same time, one thing is certain, the environment that emerges is not going to be great. The stock market will respond and will do so with a great deal of volatility. During volatile times, relying on traditional industry methods for "tactical" allocation is a recipe for suboptimal investment returns.

Why Traditional Methods Fall Short

Traditional methods can mean different things to different people. In this context, I refer to how most investors get their investment advice. Most investors get investment advice from their broker or whomever their broker gets his information. This investment opinion is the tactical overweighting or underweighting of asset classes for purposes of increasing returns or reducing negative returns. The problem is these decision makers are governed by fear just likely everybody else, but in this case, it is the fear of being wrong. If you are wrong enough times, you lose credibility, nobody listens to you, and you lose your clients. In this kind of environment, the issue for investment policy makers becomes an issue of taking the safest stance that can most easily be defended regardless of whether the tactical opinion is right or wrong. Unfortunately for investors, these investment decisions usually occur too late to add any value. In fact, most tactical decisions detract from value. Robert Prechter (2002, 226) succinctly summarizes this point:

> Throughout my career, I have always advised people not to trust a brokerage firm's "fundamental" analysts to warn you about anything. Brokerage firm analysts are notoriously poor at market timing. Besides being beholden to their corporate clients, who gives them an extreme bullish bias most of these analysts use the wrong tools. Even when they are independent thinkers, they are usually not students of market psychology and thus have no idea how to figure out when stocks are probably topping. In fact, brokerage

firm analysts are typically cheerleaders for a stock just as it
is topping out and during most of its fall.

I once worked for a firm that used to publish the results of its
tactical allocation strategy, but because the results were horrid,
they stopped publishing the data. How can you be wrong if you
have no proof?

The tactical investment decisions that are the easiest to defend
are always the ones that result in a buy recommendation well
after a significant run-up has occurred or a sell recommendation
well after a significant decline; usually by that time any value that
can be added no longer exists. When a run-up in stocks occurs,
the media will always provide ample reasons why this is the case
and why the market will go higher. As such, your broker will
always have a reason why adding risk to a portfolio was the right
thing to do. When the decision turns out to be wrong, the blame
is usually placed on some exogenous factor that was not known at
that time. This is what I mean by "safe." How can you be wrong
if you "didn't know"? The same can be said when stocks are in
decline. The media will provide ample reason why the market
is dropping and will continue to drop further. In this case, your
broker will always have a cheerleader (the media) for his decision
to reduce risk. When the market turns up, it is usually because of
some unanticipated factor. In this scenario, it becomes a matter
of saving face. Not getting out of a position when the market
is dropping is always harder to answer to than getting out of
the market only to have the market go up again. You can have
all the excuses in the world, but the bottom line in investment
management is making decisions that add value not take away
from it. The market has a law of its own, and most investment
decision makers don't or refuse to know this law. If you don't
understand this law, you will always find yourself being one step
behind. By understanding the law of the market, you are in a

good position to be right when it matters the most. More will be said on market behavior in Part 3.

Traditional methods of determining tactical asset allocation strategies fall short because they are never contrarian in nature. I define contrarian as doing something that is inherently opposite of what feels comfortable to the average investor. Using the words of legendary investor Warren Buffet, "One must buy when others are selling and sell when others are buying." This concept is extremely difficult to implement and no less difficult for "professional" investors because fear and greed are powerful emotions for everybody. All of us are comfortable buying stocks when prices are high and rising and selling when they are declining, but we need to develop an attitude that encourages us to do the opposite (Pring 1993, 1). Being contrarian doesn't always mean buying when nobody wants to buy or selling when nobody wants to sell, it also means joining an existing trend when the general "feeling" is prices are too high. In fundamentally difficult investment environments, thinking in different ways and learning to make uncomfortable decisions will be your key to investment success in the decades to come. Industry practitioners are human like everybody else and therefore are not comfortable making recommendations when they themselves lack the necessary tools and mind-set to obtain the confidence necessary in making such decisions. Hopefully, the framework and tools discussed in this book will help add value to the already difficult investment decision-making process for anybody involved in this process.

You Are Only Getting Half the Picture

The industry takes the easy way out. The general point of view for most industry practitioners is to minimize the margin for error and call it a day, but this usually results in not making important portfolio adjustments exactly at the time when portfolio adjustments are necessary. Practitioners in this fundamentally difficult environment need to offer their clients more. Almost all practitioners adapt some form of modern portfolio theory (MPT) that gives investors an asset allocation that is intended to give them a maximum return for a given level of risk. This asset allocation rarely changes.

MPT was developed between 1950 and 1970 and has been the widely accepted method of allocating financial assets. Some key assumptions of MPT are that markets are rational, markets are efficient, and more risk leads to more return. The financial crisis of 2008 has taught us that markets are not always rational, and because markets are not always rational implies that they are not always efficient. Efficient means that all available information, both historical and current, is already priced into stocks. Moreover, during times of extreme fear, more risk does not lead to more return. When investors get scared, they flee risky assets and drive up the price of less risky assets. For example, bonds outperformed stocks for the entire decade from 1999–2009; a result that runs contrary to expectation. When asset class returns run this far askew for this long, portfolio returns can be turned upside down. This is not to say that MPT is no longer valid, rather it is simply incomplete, and any investment strategy that is based solely on its tenants may reduce the chances of investors accomplishing their objectives. Many market participants are now questioning the broad framework in which their financial decisions are being made (Lo 2012, 18). As an industry, practitioners seem content to not seek solutions to a methodology that is clearly flawed. Doing nothing minimizes the chances of making a mistake, but it also maximizes the chances of fading into obsolescence. Who hires a professional simply to help them minimize mistakes? People can minimize mistakes on their own by either doing nothing or getting the asset allocation for free from the Internet and implementing an index strategy to fulfill this asset allocation. The industry has gotten away with charging hefty fees for a commoditized diversification strategy because for a long time everything was inflating and everybody was making money. Nobody cares about fees when they are making money.

When I think of most industry practitioners in this context, I often think about the challenges that golfers face. What separates good golfers from bad golfers is that the good golfers maximize their skills and make use of every opportunity to get better while bad golfers try to minimize the margin for error in their flawed swing rather than try to achieve the perfect golf swing. Just like anything else in life, if you focus only on minimizing the margin for error, especially in a methodology that is already flawed, you will lose sight of doing what it takes to get better. In this sense, industry practitioners are the same as golfers—the good practitioners minimize risk and maximize opportunity to make better investment decisions by staying the course when the market experiences a short-lived correction, being opportunistic when values are low, or making significant risk reductions when the market is ready for a long and protracted correction. The not-so good practitioner's only source of value is minimizing risk by doing nothing, which is not really a source of value because investors can do this on their own for free!

Being opportunistic when values are at significant lows or reducing risk at significant market highs does not involve a lot of trading. *Day-trading is a waste of time and valuable energy.* But an attempt should be made to identify conditions and factors that surround *protracted and sustained* moves in the market and how to profit from those moves. Being able to differentiate between a short-lived stock market correction and a correction that starts out small but gets bigger—much bigger—is at the core of successful market analysis. I have done extensive research on market trends that are protracted and long in duration and market trends that are relatively short-lived. I will discuss this research in more detail in Chapter 13.

Conclusion

Most first generation wealthy people likely achieved their wealth during the primary bull market from 1981 to 2000. But the financial collapse of 2008 changed the game. The banking environment will undergo a significant shrinkage in lending, politics will take center stage, Wall Street protests will become the norm, China's middle class will blossom, growth will occur in the emerging countries, and structural unemployment will be higher than what we have all become accustomed to.

The environment has changed, and the rules have changed. To have the greatest chance of succeeding in dealing with these changes, one must be able to cohesively combine and analyze multiple disciplines and perspectives with the end result being able to put investing in its proper perspective and thinking in different ways. These perspectives include history, psychology, politics, philosophy, technical analysis, fundamental analysis, economics, and finance. During my career, I have sought to understand all of these disciplines, how they relate to each other, and their relative importance at different points within the progression of a primary bull and primary bear market ("primary" to be defined in chapter 13). During difficult economic and sociopolitical times, it pays off to have a "general contractor" approach to financial markets because it provides one with the ability to bring together multiple specialties into a common a vision of what is occurring, and just as important, what is not occurring and how to profit from that vision. According to Empirical Research Partners in describing the state of the investment advisory industry, "A 40-year trend toward ever-greater specialization is slowly reversing, forcing managers to take on more (difficult) responsibilities."

Question and answer:

Question: You mentioned tactical asset allocation. What exactly is that again?

Answer: Tactical asset allocation is what people pay investment professionals for, to help you make money by identifying market imperfections and to advise you on how you can either profit from those imperfections or reduce risk. In difficult economic, political, and business environments, tactical asset allocation is an important source of value. But tactical asset allocation is something that is difficult to do successfully and consistently. Unfortunately, the degree of expertise in this area varies widely within the investment industry; therefore, you must choose your advisor wisely or learn how to do it on your own.

Chapter 4

A FRAMEWORK

Similar to entrepreneurs who have to prepare a business plan that details their market environment and how they plan to profit in that environment, successful investors must understand the environment in which they are operating. In the following seven chapters, I will illustrate and provide a framework to observe, understand, and predict sociopolitical and economic trends. Part of this framework includes key elements that cause change, the kinds of change that the stock market finds important. Some of these elements include how to know when equilibrium-changing events may be occurring, the role that ideas play as a political weapon, and the role that economic philosophies play in shaping economic policy. *A broad understanding of the interplay between society, politics, and economics serves as the domain in which markets operate, and without a thorough understanding of them, it is extremely difficult to obtain the perspective necessary to achieve long-term investment success.*

Understanding the current macro environment and the events leading up to it is a prerequisite for having a sense of how social, economic, financial, political, and international events will unfold in the future. Having an understanding of the current macro environment, however, does not mean that one will know the exact course of future events or if that understanding is the correct interpretation of what is actually occurring; nonetheless, it is crucial as it allows one to be in a better position to know when to change investment strategy as events unfold in real time. For example, in August of 2008, right after the takeover of Bear Stearns by JP Morgan and right after the Housing and Economic Recovery Act of 2008 was signed into law, I expected the market to engineer its own soft landing. After all, much of the damage had already been done (or so I thought), and monetary and fiscal stimulus were very accommodative. My thought process was that consumer and business expectations were so low for so long that the market would engineer its own soft landing. In addition, valuations were fair, and banks had already written off hundreds of billions of dollars. However, the Lehman bankruptcy in September of 2008 dealt a huge blow to the psyche of every consumer, business, bank, investor, and policy maker in the world. Knowing that the psychological effect of this bankruptcy (the largest bankruptcy on record) would have a lasting effect, I decided to change course. I became much more defensive.

According to Robert Gilpin (2001, 41), "Achievement of our goal of comprehending the international political economy functions will probably always be elusive no matter how hard we work to improve the study of the international political economy." No matter how elusive this comprehension may be, an attempt to understand the current sociopolitical and economic environment should be made.

An interdisciplinary approach to understanding the world in which we live is crucial. Economic theories alone are not sufficient for an understanding of developments and their significance for economic and political affairs. One must also draw upon ideas and insights from history, political science, and other social sciences (Gilpin 2001, 12). According to Victor Sperandeo (2001, 109-110):

> A huge part of successful speculation and investment now rests on anticipating the nature and effects of government fiscal policy, monetary policy, and interventionist legislation on specific markets and on the general business

cycle. Our economy operates according to market principles, but the government sets the stage—and it's a secret, rotating stage subject to change at any moment. But if you understand the errors in the economic theory that motivate the stage managers you can anticipate the new set and position yourself to act profitably. Therefore, understanding economics has *everything* to do with successful speculation and investment; it provides the foundation for any good system of market forecasting.

The main drivers of all economic activity are consumers, businesses, government, investors, and financial intermediaries. Ask yourself how consumers, businesses, government, investors, and financial intermediaries are likely to behave. What are their fears? How are they likely to think? How are they likely to feel? What are their trade-offs? The answers to these questions are front and center to understanding the environment we are in. The next seven chapters provide a context and framework for answering these types of questions. To this end, the following chapters will expand on these concepts:

- Having a point of reference and importance of learning from history
- Economic equilibriums
- Cash, credit, banking, and the Fed
- Politics—the battle for ideas
- Economic philosophies
- Secular trends
- Fundamentals of stock valuation

If you are running or have ever run a business or a nonprofit organization, you can appreciate the importance of having a reference point and learning from history. Every entity that wants to exist as a going concern is always going to have changing management teams. Every management team has its opinion of what needs to be done to fix things. However, making these decisions without understanding the history of the organization and how it came to be can be disastrous. What if the changes are too radical? What if the people and the culture are not able to support these changes? How fast can the changes be made without things falling apart? What about customers? How are they likely to perceive these changes? The same can be said about investing in financial markets that are a reflection of overall business conditions and the entities and people involved in shaping these conditions. How can you anticipate and forecast future behavior if you don't know where you've been? In chapter 5, I will discuss how you can define a point of reference and use the experiences of history to help you make smarter investment decisions.

There are certain defining moments in any business or nonprofit organization. These moments are what I call "aha" moments that say unequivocally that change and any risk of change is necessary and that operating "business as usual" is no longer acceptable. These are equilibrium-changing moments. Equilibrium-changing moments don't happen that often, but when they do, they can make big waves throughout an organization. According to Jim Smith, Chief Logistics Officer for Avnet, "Structure always follows strategy." When strategies, out of necessity change, old structures need to be torn down, and new structures to support the new strategies are constructed. This process when magnified to scales of an entire country or an entire world can lead to significant opportunities if you can identify them in advance. Chapter 6 will cover how to spot changes in economic equilibriums.

Every single body of life needs energy to survive. The same can be said for an entire economy, it must have energy if it is to exist and thrive. Cash and credit is the energy any economy must have if it is to exist. Just like human energy levels rise and fall depending on external factors such as blood sugar levels and level of activity, economic activity, in large part, depend on cash and credit. If you want to make money in financial markets, you must first understand the role that credit plays in the economy. Chapter 7 discusses the essential factors of what causes cash and credit to expand, contract, or otherwise change.

If you have ever been part of a leadership or management team, you can attest to the importance of politics in the role that people play in shaping outcomes. For the lay person, it is impossible to know all the bribes and corruption that go on behind the scenes. But one thing is certain, the political stage in which many decisions are made results in an ideology that is thrown out and a new one put in its place. In chapter 8, I will discuss the political process in shaping ideas and how this process can affect your mind-set and decisions about investing.

Some business themes of the past twenty years include total quality management, employee empowerment, technology, expansion, "rightsizing," risk management, regulation, and expense control. Notice the ebb and flow from growth to contraction and the form that it takes. Every single era of business from expansion to contraction is defined by an idea or a philosophy that shapes all other decisions. In the growth phase, employees are cherished and empowered. In the contraction phase, employees need to be controlled and regulated. The same can be said for economic philosophies that have shaped every significant time in American history. When the economy is doing well, businesses need to be empowered, and when the economy collapses because somehow capitalism has failed us, businesses need to be regulated. Chapter 9 discusses several economic philosophies that have shaped American ideology and will likely have an influence again in the future. Understand these philosophies, and you will understand how to best position your investment portfolio accordingly.

Every defining and equilibrium-changing era that any going-concern entity goes through usually does so because of changes in social, demographic, and economic conditions that are titanic in size. One needs to have a sense of how these long-term secular trends will unfold and the rate in which they unfold. I cover some of these secular trends in chapter 10.

Part 2 concludes with understanding the fundamentals of stock valuation. Every corporation has to balance the need to grow, manage risk, and sustain its current business. How managers balance these competing objectives ultimately determines its value to investors. The same can be said for the stock market. Chapter 11 sketches a broad overview of how stocks are valued.

Chapter 5

HAVING A POINT OF REFERENCE—IMPORTANCE OF HAVING A HISTORICAL PERSPECTIVE

A point of reference is a business cycle peak or trough that can be easily identified. Although a point of reference cannot be identified until after the fact, sometimes well after the fact, does not diminish its usefulness. A point of reference is important because it allows investors a starting point to draw conclusions on how sociopolitical and economic conditions may change. The importance of having a point of reference is similar to the importance of having a starting point to map directions from. It is impossible to obtain a travel route without a starting point. Using the financial collapse of 2008 as a reference point, for example, one can surmise the following:

- Consumers will de-lever (pay down debt) for a long time
- Politicians will fight and blame each other, causing public anxiety
- At some point a reversal of the stimulation is necessary
- Bank lending will be subdued
- Regulation will increase

- Companies will benefit from abnormally low financing rates
- A disequilibrium exists between the supply and demand for money and where interest rates actually are. At some point rates will have to rise.

Being able to understand the political, economic, and social progression following a reference period is a powerful analytical tool. In addition, one must also understand that financial markets will behave in unique and disconnected ways during and following reference points. The market will overshoot to the downside, overshoot to the upside, go up when everyone thinks it should go down, and go down when everyone thinks it should go up. We will discuss market behavior more in Part 3.

Reference points occur as the economy is ready to enter a recession (cycle peaks) or during periods when the economy is bottoming and coming out of a recession (cycle troughs). The National Bureau of Economic Research (NBER) usually announces the beginning and end of recessions many months after a recession starts and ends respectively. However, economists' consensus of the end and beginning of recessions are usually provided many months before NBER. Some examples of key business cycle peak reference points include the recessions of December 2007, March of 2001, and August of 1929. Examples of key business cycle bottom reference points include the economic recoveries of August 2009, November 1982, and March 1933.

Business cycle peaks and troughs, and therefore reference points, vary in their magnitude. Some cycle peaks and troughs have small implications and some have large implications for the economy and the stock market. Whether business cycle peaks or troughs have small or large economic and market implications depend on the existence of one or more of the following sociopolitical and economic conditions:

- Recession
- Asset bubble
- Financial crisis
- Hyperinflation
- Inflation
- Disinflation
- Deflation
- Stagflation
- Trough war
- Peak war
- Regulation
- Deregulation
- Productivity

The first step in trying to predict the natural progression of social mood, politics, and the economy is to identify which of the above conditions were characteristic of the reference point. Cycle peaks with large implications usually are accompanied by several of these conditions occurring simultaneously, such as a deep recession, asset bubble, financial crisis, and deflation. Recoveries from cycle troughs that were caused by these conditions are equally powerful.

Cycle peaks and troughs with smaller implications usually involve only one or two of these conditions. For example, the recession from July 1990 to March 1991 can be considered milder than the average recession despite the Savings and Loans (S&L) crisis and the Persian Gulf War. The 1990–91 recession was shorter than most of the previous postwar recessions and characterized by proportionately fewer job losses. Officially, this recession lasted eight months, in contrast to an average duration of eleven months for previous recessions, and employment fell 1.0 percent, significantly less than the average drop of 2.5 percent.[4] The S&L crisis, which was not truly systemic, affected a subsector within an otherwise functioning large financial market.[5] Because this reference point was a recession that was much milder than the typical recession and because the S&L crisis was well contained, the DJIA declined only 15 percent that lasted only a little over four months.

The financial and economic collapse of 2008 resulted in a devastating 50 percent drop for the DJIA, but it provides a valuable point of reference. During this crisis, world markets experienced an asset bubble (real estate), financial crisis, and deep recession all occurring at the same time and negatively feeding off each other. Having all three of these conditions occur at once is not something that happens often. The question that needs to be answered is how does the world move forward given the psychological and economic devastation caused by this financial collapse? How will consumers respond? How will businesses respond? How will the government respond? How will banks respond? How will investors respond? Careful study of sociopolitical and economic conditions within a historical context can help provide clues to answering these questions. The reason why you hear so much about the Great Depression in the context of describing the financial collapse of 2008 is because that was the last time the United States experienced a recession, financial collapse, and asset bubble that were all occurring simultaneously. The primary bear market that started in March 2000 took the DJIA down 34 percent and consisted of an asset bubble (tech stocks) and a recession, but no systematic financial collapse. The DJIA went on to make a new high later that decade.

Importance of a Having a Historical Perspective

Having a point of reference, understanding the conditions that surround it, and putting that point of reference in a historical context can provide invaluable guidance in understanding how these conditions may affect the future behavior of key participants within the international political economy. Mark Twain once said, "History does not repeat; it rhymes." Events and the people behind them do not repeat, but the magnitude of events does repeat. For example, I would argue that the canals of the midnineteenth century, the railways of the late nineteenth century and early twentieth century, and the supply-chain revolution of the late twentieth century all had a similar impact on social, political, and business spheres; all three inventions were different, but they all served to connect commerce from remote locations.

Policy makers are notorious for their study of history. A quick review of almost every major university's methodology in international policy, economics, business, and international relations courses will show extensive use of case studies of actual problems that had occurred in the past. As a result, domestic and foreign policy may not be the same today as it was in the past given similar social, political, and business stimuli due the learning and experience that came about as a result of studying the prior episode. The idea is to know how policies may differ and how that difference will affect consumers, businesses, government, investors, and the financial system. For example, policy makers during the financial crisis of 2008 did not repeat the same policy mistakes that had occurred during the Great Depression. What matters is how economic or foreign policy may change based on learning of the past. *Investors need to be careful about assuming that today's events are going to transpire exactly like they had in the past.*

Having knowledge of how present-day economic policies may change relative to policies of the past given similar conditions provides one with insight into how important financial variables such as short-term rates, long-term rates, currency valuation, and inflation may change in response. Many industry professionals and retail investors fall into the trap of using wrong reference points. For example, those who have attempted to put the 2008 financial and economic crisis into a historical perspective have cited 1933, 1937, 1974, 1981, and 1991 as precedents. 1933 was the beginning of the recovery *following* the Great Depression, 1937 was the first recession following the recovery that started in 1933, 1974 was a recession caused by an oil crisis, 1981 was a recession caused by tight monetary policy aimed at bringing down inflation, and 1991 was a mild recession that occurred as a result of the credit contraction associated with the Savings and Loan Crisis and the U.S. invasion of Iraq. Although the financial crisis of 2008 does have some commonalities with each of those periods, the only true precedent in terms of social, economic, business, and political conditions is the Great Depression that started in 1929. One reason why other periods have been cited as precedents is due to similarities in financial variables. For example, 1974 had near hyperinflation (there was much concern that the United States would have hyperinflation as a result of the multiple rounds of quantitative easing following the financial collapse of 2008) and 1991 had a drastic devaluation in commercial real estate (so did the financial collapse of 2008).

There are a couple notable examples of how policy makers have learned from past episodes of similar circumstances. Throughout the Great Depression, US policy makers were raising interest rates to counter the raising of interest rates in Great Britain and to help stop the outflow of gold. In Japan, during the 1980s, it took policy makers seventeen months to ease credit conditions after their commercial real estate bubble. Japan is now in the midst of twenty years of stagnation. Mistakes of the magnitude seen in Japan in the 1980s and the United States in the 1930s have not been repeated since, at least not in the United States. The financial collapse of 2008 was the closest event to the Great Depression since 1929, but policy makers were quick to act with swift monetary and fiscal stimulus. The Federal Reserve, through its Troubled Asset Relief Program (TARP) and various rounds of quantitative easing, were in stark contrast to the monetary and fiscal tightening that had occurred during the Great Depression. Additionally, there was much talk about the United States encountering a multidecade period of deflation similar to Japan after their housing market bubble in the late 1980s. The last thing US policy makers want is to be ridiculed by repeating the same mistakes that had happened in the past.

Just like partying too hard and drinking too much can cause a serious hangover, too much excess credit and binge spending will also lead to an economic hangover. Whether taxes are raised or interest rates are raised, as was the case during the Great Depression, or rates are dropped to zero and money is created through quantitative easing (chapter 7 will discuss quantitative easing), as was the case during the financial collapse of 2008, the piper still needs to be paid. Excesses still needed to be unwound. Rather than take the pain all at once as was the case during the Great Depression, we have made our hangover less severe but have extended its duration and potentially created unintended consequences in the process. These unintended consequences could include a nasty bout with inflation.

In sum, despite the fact that events and personalities do not repeat themselves, there are certain aspects of human nature that does repeat. *Politics will always be politics, fear will always be fear, greed will always be greed, people will always be impatient, short-term sacrifices are rarely made for the benefit of the longer term, and people and states will always have a need for security.* The study of history provides investors with a sense of how these various aspects of human nature have a tendency to repeat in differing contexts. Ralph Nelson Elliott recognized early on these repetitive human emotional and cognitive tendencies. Robert Prechter and A.J. Frost have furthered the study of Elliott and labeled the body of work as the Wave Principle. The Wave Principle is governed by man's social nature, and since he has such a nature, its expression generates forms (Prechter and Frost 2005, 21). *History helps one to understand how sociopolitical conditions may take shape given a reference point in which to craft these conclusions from.*

Question and answer

Question: I keep listening to this guy who has been prognosticating that the DJIA is going to drop back into the 9,000 (January 2012 while the DJIA was at 12,600) area within the next few weeks. What he is saying makes a lot of sense in that what he sees is similar to what the market was doing in March of 2000 and October of 2007. Before the market fell apart, they showed signs of rolling over and that is what he sees now. I want to retire, and I don't have enough right now to retire the way I want to. What should I do? Should I try to get out of the market before this happens?

Answer: One thing to keep in mind is that the Tech Wreck of March 2000 consisted of an asset bubble with tech stocks, extremely high market valuations, and a recession that followed. The financial collapse of 2008 consisted of an asset bubble with real estate, a financial collapse, and deep recession occurring all at once. Valuations are much lower than the historical average and there is no asset bubble in sight. The reference points of the two instances you mentioned just aren't characteristic of what is happening now. Right now I would stay the course.

Chapter 6

THINKING IN TERMS OF EQUILIBRIUM

The stock market moves with knee-jerk reaction to daily events, but very few of these events change the equilibrium between supply and demand. Separating this noise from the fundamentals that truly affect aggregate supply and demand is at the heart of understanding the environment in which the market operates and is also a key component of spotting early turning points in the market. Intermediate and primary moves in the stock market are usually accompanied by equilibrium-changing events or perceptions, either good or bad, of equilibrium-changing events. Equilibrium means that no economic actor has an incentive to change his or her behavior, and the costs and benefits of the existing situation are judged to have achieved the best balance that an individual could reasonably expect. In other words, equilibrium occurs when supply equals demand. Disequilibrium occurs when the supply-demand relationship becomes out of alignment. *Economists use the term "disequilibrium" to mean any change in demand, opportunities, or relative prices that gives an economic actor an incentive to change his or her behavior in order to increase his or her gains or decrease his or her costs* (Gilpin 2001, 55). The importance of thinking in equilibrium terms helps one to sort out the noise and filter out the events that are not significant enough to create a change to a new equilibrium.

Between 2003 and 2007, credit conditions were extremely easy as the Fed reduced interest rates to 1 percent by the middle of 2003 to fight off the unwinding that occurred as a result of the Tech Wreck of 2000. The liquidity generated by easy credit conditions was directed toward residential and commercial real estate. In many parts of California, Arizona, Nevada, and Florida, real estate values doubled between 2004 and 2006. The rapid increase in real estate valuations created massive borrowing on home equity lines of credit. The massive expansion of home equity lines of credit fueled consumer spending, which in turn resulted in massive expansion in infrastructure—office space, retail space, property, plant, and equipment—to meet this demand. Unfortunately, the real estate collapse stopped this unsustainable demand dead in its tracks; however, the infrastructure (the supply) had already been constructed or was in the process of being constructed. The unsustainable demand that resulted from rising real estate values and easy credit conditions caused a disequilibrium that occurred between 2003 and 2007 as consumers increased consumption, financial companies increased profit through lending, investors wanted to make a quick buck, and businesses wanted to play its part.

Consumers changed their behavior significantly by picking up their rate of spending. As demand increased so did the need for supply of infrastructure. The new supply-demand relationship was higher than the previous supply-demand equilibrium. However, significant demand shrinkage and financial collapse of 2008 created a new equilibrium to form that dropped much lower than the previous equilibrium. Demand shrunk as unemployment increased from 4.8 percent to 9.8 percent between October 2007 and October 2009. But supply shrunk as well, resulting in a new supply-demand relationship. I sat in countless meetings over this two-year time period where clients would march on about a nascent recovery and high unemployment. In terms of how this situation affected the stock market, it was not a matter of how bad things were; it was a matter of whether a new equilibrium was in the process of forming. If a new equilibrium was in the process of forming, then the main issue at hand would have been how the market would recover from that point, not a matter of how dismal things were or how dismal things felt. In other words, if the economy was at a new point of equilibrium in the first half of 2009 and market prices had already factored that in, then it would have been worthwhile for investors to get some cash committed to equities (or not sell completely out) despite the troubles of that time.

Thinking in terms of equilibrium is essential, but it is also very difficult for one to know if the economic system is at a new equilibrium. The concept of equilibrium is a powerful analytic tool. Yet this concept can also be quite misleading. Economists generally use the term as if they really could determine at any particular moment whether or not equilibrium actually exists in a particular market (Gilpin 2001, 56). *As such, it is better for investors to understand the "feel" of the process of equilibrium formation and to not get bogged down in the details of specifically defining the precise point of equilibrium.*

What Causes Changes in Economic Equilibrium?

There is no one factor that causes the economy to change equilibrium between aggregate supply and aggregate demand. Equilibrium changes or disequilibrium occurs because of a change in social and economic conditions that causes people and businesses to change their behavior in order to maximize gains, minimize losses, increase consumption, or decrease consumption. This change in condition and human behavior occur slowly over time.

For example, for the period 2006 to 2010, the supply of real estate was going up and the demand was going down. As a result, the equilibrium between supply and demand had encountered a catastrophic drop. But between the middle of 2010 and the beginning of 2012, a slow shift began to emerge. Real estate prices began the process of forming a bottom, albeit at a low equilibrium.

Real estate values and stock market values diverged for nearly three years from March 2009 to December 2011. The stock market was going up, but real estate values were going down. Since March of 2009, the DJIA was up nearly 90 percent while the average single family home price was down 5 percent according to the Case Shiller Housing Index. However, the eighteen months ended February 2012, an equilibrium change began to take shape as key actors in the economy began to change their behaviors. New home and existing home sales were at six months of supply (this means at current demand, it would take six months to work off the inventory), which was down from eleven months supply two years earlier. Average home prices were showing a rapid reduction in their rate of decline and demand was picking up

Here is how the real estate market created a directional upward change in equilibrium. Investors, seeing that real estate values were at historic levels of affordability and seeing that demand for rental properties was increasing, were buying rental properties in bulk, sometimes twenty to thirty houses at a time. Investors in rental homes *changed their behavior* because values were down to such attractive levels that it was hard to pass them up. At the same time, banks were reluctant to foreclose on defaulted borrowers because they did not want to flood the market with supply. As a result, housing prices started to stabilize, albeit at very low levels. Seeing this stabilization, savvy real estate investors, called "flippers," started buying properties for fractions of their loan amount, fixed them up, and resold them at much higher prices. All the sudden real estate prices were reset at higher levels. Banks, beginning to see that home values were stabilizing, had more confidence to lend money. The second half of 2011 saw the first six-month net increase in bank credit since 2006. More lending caused the velocity of money to increase and then the next thing you knew there was a self-sustaining real estate recovery.

This equilibrium-changing process all started because real estate investors were looking for cheap rental properties. This provided the first sign that there was some demand for real estate. Then, real estate flippers emerged on the stage and added another layer of demand. All the while, banks were controlling supply. Real estate prices stabilized, which gave banks the confidence to lend again. This real estate example is a good illustration of how a positive disequilibrium occurred and the seeds planted for a new and higher equilibrium to form. Spotting in advance the formation of these equilibriums can be a very profitable endeavor.

The importance of a recovery in real estate to the environment that defined 2012 was very important for so many sectors of the economy, especially banking. Without a recovery in real estate, no matter how small, banks will not lend; and if banks don't lend, the economy will stall.

Question and answer

Question: The unemployment rate is north of 10 percent, and when you consider the people who are so discouraged that they are not looking for work, this number is probably north of 16 percent. I feel in order for us to see any improvement in the economy, we need to see improvement in employment. What do you think?

Answer: I agree that unemployment is high and probably even higher when you take into consideration the discouraged worker. There is no doubt the demand has shrunk; after all, people are losing their jobs. But supply has shrunk to. You don't have to drive too far to see once-filled

---

commercial and retail space. Businesses that supply products and services have shrunk to meet the reduced demand. The environment is definitely not great, but the important thing is whether we are approaching a new equilibrium between supply and demand. And if so, the key question is how do we move forward from here? Consumers have been deleveraging (paying down bills) for the past eighteen months and have put off buying things they would have otherwise bought if the economic environment were more normal. I think that the expectation has been set so low that it will not take much from these levels to have some positive surprises. I believe the economy moves forward cautiously.

Question and answer

Question: The economy created a new equilibrium in 2009, one that was lower than the previous equilibrium between supply and demand. What do you think will cause the next equilibrium change where economic actors will have an incentive to change their behavior to maximize profits or minimize losses?

Answer: 2012 saw a continuation of what started in July of 2009, which was an increase in consumer spending, albeit at a slow pace. So the question is, what will cause a disequilibrium where people reduce their spending? Higher interest rates and higher taxes are equilibrium-changing events that will cause people to reduce their spending. Fiscal and monetary policies have been very accommodative because they can be without adverse effects. The world is still willing to hold and continue to buy US Treasury bonds despite the fiscal deficits and inflationary policies. However, when inflation becomes a serious threat, US policy makers are going to have to make a tough choice, one they will have to tighten fiscal policy and raise rates or risk a run on the US dollar as foreign investors will flee US-dollar denominated assets. Higher taxes and higher interest rates will cause people to spend less, which will likely be the cause of the next recession. However, a continuation of fiscal imbalance and inflationary policies will lead to foreign investors dumping US treasury bonds, which will lead to weakness in the dollar and hyperinflation. When faced with these two choices, the lesser of two evils will prevail and that is to drive the domestic economy into a recession rather than risk a complete loss of faith in US-dollar denominated assets.

Question and answer

Question: You stated an interesting point, "Intermediate and primary moves in the stock market are usually accompanied by equilibrium changing events or perceptions, either good or bad, of equilibrium-changing events." I hear a lot about self-fulfilling prophecies and how people can create their own reality, and in the process, if enough people think the same way, can alter the reality of others in good or bad ways. Although I feel good about the economy, I am afraid for my investments because if people get scared with the austere events that have occurred in Europe they will sell and drive prices down and this could create a self-fulfilling prophecy where price drops lead to further price drops. What are your thoughts?

Answer: Market corrections based on a perception that is not accurate don't last that long. I call these risk-based corrections where the market corrects due to a perceived level of risk that does not come true. Usually, these corrections are not indicative of a directional change in equilibrium, they just seem to. Sustained and protracted moves in the market, however, are usually indicative of a change in equilibrium. With regard to Europe, stock market and bond market values have already suffered a significant drop and are currently reflecting complete anarchy and breakup of the euro currency. Here in the United States, the stock market is flat for the year. I think the issues in Europe are already priced in to the market, thus any further decline may be pricing in a collapse in the euro currency that I don't believe will happen.

I would also add that you don't really know if a perception is false or not until after the fact. As they say, hindsight is twenty-twenty. However, careful study of stock market behavior and the duration of primary bull and bear markets can provide some clues to whether the market is just correcting or about ready to start a long and protracted move. Chapter 13 discusses the stock market's historical tendencies.

Chapter 7

MONEY, BANKING, CREDIT, AND THE FED

If the main actors of the economy—consumers, businesses, investors, banks, and government—are akin to the various body parts of the human anatomy, then cash and credit is akin to the bloodstream that flows through it. Just like the body will die without blood, the economy will die without cash and credit. It is almost impossible to understand the current macro environment without understanding how cash, credit, banking, and the Fed all fit into the picture. The purpose of this chapter is to define, discuss, and recognize how cash and credit work in a complex and specialized economy by illustrating many monetarily based concepts that were widely discussed and debated during the financial crisis of 2008 and will undoubtedly resurface at some point in time in the future.

A Brief History of Our Monetary System

During the midnineteenth century, the United States was on a true gold standard where the growth of US-denominated notes could only grow to the extent of the gold stock. The temporary suspension of this linkage came during the Civil War when war-related expenses resulted in an increase in US-denominated notes that outpaced the growth and availability of gold. The link between dollars (greenbacks as they were called at the time) and gold—known as specie resumption—came back into vogue again in 1873 (officially specie resumption occurred in 1879, but the US economy began its preparation for that in 1873), an event that caused what was known as the "Great Depression of the 1870s."

The next one hundred years, as wars became the norm, there was no chance that dollar growth could be confined to the growth in gold. The period from 1879 to 1914 was known as the Classical Gold Standard where most industrial countries including the United States were firmly linked to gold. After specie resumption occurred successfully in 1879, the gold premium to greenbacks fell to par and the appreciated greenback promoted confidence in the gold-backed dollar (Rothbard 2005, 160). However, during and after World War I, the monetary system based on the gold standard was in jeopardy. Several Developments associated with the First World War reduced the relevance of the gold standard model (Aliber 2002, 43). The First World War was the first major war since the dollar was once again pegged to gold. History has shown that during inflationary times, strict adherence to a gold standard is extremely difficult. At the beginning of the First World War, most European countries left the gold standard since their rates of inflation were much higher than the US inflation rate; indeed, the US dollar was the only major currency that remained convertible to gold. The benefit of World War I, if there is to be any benefit at all, is that the United States emerged militaristically and economically more powerful than any other country at that time. After the First World War, the US economy was about as large as the combined economies of the ten next largest countries—a much more dominant position in the world economy than Great Britain had ever enjoyed (Aliber 2002, 44).

The period between 1917 and 1944 was a period of very loose connections between major currencies and gold. After World War I, many European countries tried to get back on to the gold standard at their prewar ratios; however this undertaking proved too difficult and costly for many countries to maintain. By 1931, most major countries in Europe went off the gold standard. During the Great Depression, much fear was spread regarding the outflow of gold from the United States. As such, in 1933, President Franklin D. Roosevelt changed the parity from $20.67 to $35.

Toward the end of World War II in 1944, world leaders met in New Hampshire to discuss a more permanent international monetary arrangement that would end the cycle of deflation, to inflation, to hyperinflation that had plagued much of the world in the previous seventy-five years. This arrangement was known as Bretton Woods. It obligated member countries to convert foreign official holdings of their gold at certain par levels. However, since most of the world's gold was in the United States, many countries simply pegged their currencies to the dollar, thus *making the dollar the world's defacto currency.*[6] Bretton Woods maintained itself until 1971, when President Nixon officially abandoned the US dollar's linkage to gold. As a result, most other countries' currencies were allowed to float against the dollar, an arrangement that still exists today.

Because much of the world was pegged to the dollar and the dollar had delinked itself from any relationship to gold despite multiple failed attempts—Classic Gold Standard and Bretton Woods—to stay united, *the purpose of gold in the world monetary system evaporated.*

Question and answer

Question: It sounds like we have gone through various cycles throughout history where gold has played a significant role in the monetary system and at other times has not. Do you think we will go back on any type of gold standard again?

Answer: We have been completely off the gold standard for over forty years. If you look back in history, you will see that the gold standard has always been popular after a period of hyper-inflationary crisis. Moreover, the gold standard has always been unpopular during periods of crisis, such as war that required more monetary stimulus. Because productivity and technological advancement has been so strong over the past few decades, hyperinflation has not been a real threat. But I know that there are enough people who fear inflation because of all the quantitative easing that has taken place over the past few years.

But I think that a reversal of the stimulus through increases in interest rates and potentially some tightening fiscal policy may be enough to bring any fear of inflation back down again. Although it is hard to predict too far out with regard to any monetary arrangements, I believe that a gold standard is not in the cards any time soon. There was a good article on gold in the April 24th, 2012 issue of USA Today, which said, "on a practical level, there is not enough gold in the world to return to a gold standard – and no one else in the world is on the gold standard. By tying the value of the dollar to gold, the government cedes control of monetary policy, making it unable to increase the money supply in times of economic crisis."[7]

The Fed

The Fed is the nation's central bank. The Federal Reserve System was established by Congress in 1913, following the banking crisis of 1907. It was hoped that the Federal Reserve System would prevent a repetition of such disasters (Bernstein 2008, 69). Virtually every country has a central bank. The purpose of the Fed is to help control the money supply through various tools, the most common of which is through open market operations (to be discussed later). In addition, the Fed has historically served as the lender of last resort during situations of financial panic. The Fed has a chairman who serves as its primary figure head. A list of Fed Chairmen (from most recent) includes Ben Bernanke, Alan Greenspan, and Paul Volcker.

Over time, the purpose and significance of the Fed has changed from its original inception back in 1913. Some would site that the Fed now has multiple mandates: lender of last resort, control of money supply, maintain full employment, target interest rates, target inflation rates, etc. In a financial crisis, the Fed has four main tasks: to keep the banking system liquid, to maintain the public's confidence in banks, to maintain the market's faith in the value of treasury securities, which constitute its own reserves, and to maintain the integrity of the dollar relative to other currencies since dollars are the basis of the Fed's power (Prechter 2002, 131). In a system-wide financial crisis, these goals will conflict. If the Fed chooses to favor any of these goals, the others will be compromised. Keeping the banking system liquid and maintaining the public's confidence in banks require the Fed to stimulate credit by reducing interest rates, trading "dead assets" (like Bear Stearns subprime mortgage debt) for good money, reducing the discount rate, and taking in other less credit-worthy collateral for loans. All these things serve to increase credit and the money supply, thus adding to the outstanding dollars, which increases inflation as there are more dollars chasing the same basket of goods. In doing so, the Fed reduces the value of its own balance sheet and thus compromises the value of the dollar.

How It All Works

Say Congress needs $1 billion to pay for a war. Congress will tap the Department of Treasury on the shoulder and ask them to issue $1 billion worth of treasury bonds. Then banks, both domestic and foreign, will buy these bonds. Now, Congress has the money it needs to pay for military salaries, guns, and ammunition. At this point, no money is being created because of the match of savers and borrowers. The purchase of these new bonds came from savings that already existed. How then, does money come into existence?

The next step, which involves the Fed, is the step where money is created. The Fed, through its normal process of open-market operations and quantitative easing (to be discussed later), will buy these bonds from banks and take them as assets on their balance sheet. Banks now have more cash to lend out. Well, how did the Fed get the money to buy these assets from the banks to begin with? The answer is with the stroke of a pen. Because, initially, Congress needed the money to pay for a war and did so through a $1 billion bond issuance that ultimately landed on the Fed's balance sheet, money is considered to be "loaned into existence"[8] through the commercial banking system. All money created is backed by debt.

Chris Martenson in his DVD *Crash Course* quotes the Boston Federal Reserve, "When you write a check there must be sufficient funds in our account to cover the check, but when the Federal Reserve writes a check there is no bank deposit on which that check is drawn. When the Federal Reserve writes a check it is creating money."[9]

Question and answer

Question: Why doesn't the government use the money it prints to pay off its own debt?

Answer: Money supply expansion occurs through the banking system and is done so through the issuance of new credit. In reality, the government does issue new debt that is purchased by the Fed or bought by the public. Some of this debt can be used to pay off its old and maturing debt. But the government cannot just create money that is not backed by some kind of debt obligation to pay off its existing debt. If they could do so, they would have done so a long time ago. If they ever tried to do such a thing, the international community would abandon all US-denominated assets because hyperinflation would result.

The Fractional Reserve Banking System

The fractional reserve banking system characterizes all industrial countries across the world and has been around in one form or another for over 150 years. To illustrate, suppose you deposit $10,000 into your commercial bank account, the bank lends out 90 percent (assuming a 10 percent reserve requirement) or $9,000 and keeps the remaining $1,000 on reserve to help meet redemptions of demand deposits. The borrower of this $9,000 then deposits that into his commercial bank account. This bank loans out $8,100 and keeps the other $900 on reserve. This bank, in turn, loans out this $7,290 and keeps the remaining $810 on reserve. If you continued this process until all loanable dollars are loaned out, you will see that with an initial $10,000 deposit with a 10 percent reserve requirement, you can expand the money supply by a factor of 9 (assuming you continue in the above calculations until all loanable dollars are lent out). You may have also caught on, that under a fractional reserve banking system, there is not enough cash on hand if everybody went to the banks to demand their money in cash. After all, in this example, the banks collectively only started with $10,000. The process also works in reverse, when loans are paid off; this takes money out of the monetary system.

The Myth about Printing Money

Let's clarify the process of what many people refer to as *printing money*. I've met with many clients and people at seminars that I have given that have expressed concern over the politically driven anxiety over the concept of printing money and the misconception that hoards of cash are just dropped from a helicopter. Although the government does have the authority to mint new bills and coins, doing so instead of raising taxes or issuing debt—with a corresponding interest payment—is not something the government wants to do since this practice is catastrophically inflationary and investors would lose all confidence in dollar-denominated assets. This is what happened in Germany after World War I to pay for its war reparations. Because inflation was so rampant in Germany after World War I, people demanded to be paid every day since prices were rising so rapidly and they wanted to make purchases at lower prices today than pay higher prices tomorrow.

Eventually, new bills had to be created that were in larger, much larger, denominations than the old bills. Once there was a man with hoards of German marks in his wheelbarrow who stopped at a stoplight waiting to cross the road. He turned away for a minute, and when he turned back, his wheelbarrow was gone and all his currency was left on the sidewalk. Of course this is a fictitious story, but the point is clear: you can't just "print" money. Another example occurred in Yugoslavia in the early 1990s where Between October 1, 1993, and January 24, 1995, prices increased by 5 quadrillion percent. This number is a five with fifteen zeroes after it. The social structure began to collapse. Thieves robbed hospitals and clinics of scarce pharmaceuticals and then sold them in front of the same places they robbed. The railway workers went on strike and closed down Yugoslavia's rail system.[10] There is a big difference between printing money and money creation. Although both processes are inflationary, the latter is the more acceptable means of increasing the money supply as it is the process that is based on the fractional reserve banking system and is less inflationary than the type of money printing that occurred in Germany after WWI and Yugoslavia in the early 1990s. *The process that we know of as "printing money" occurs through the commercial banking system and is done through the creation of credit as discussed earlier.*

Quantitative Easing—What Is It?

When the Fed expands its balance sheet, it is buying assets in the open market in what is known as quantitative easing. Typically, quantitative easing occurs when interests are near 0 percent and the assets purchased are securities other than short-term treasury bonds. For example, in 2009 the Fed committed to over $1 trillion dollars of asset purchases that consisted of longer dated treasuries, mortgage-backed securities, and debt instruments of the government-sponsored entities of Fannie Mae and Freddie Mac. When these assets are purchased by the Fed, the seller's bank reserves get credited and the bank, in turn, credits the seller's deposit account. Just like magic, credit is created because now the bank has more cash to lend than it had prior to the asset purchase. Yes, it is true that the seller of the security can take this money out of the account and spend it. But the seller's cash used to purchase his next widget is then deposited into the buyer's bank. The buyer's bank can then lend this money out. It does not matter what happens after the initial sale of the security; the key to this transaction is that the security sale took place with the Fed, as if it had a magic wand, as the buyer who simply credits the seller's bank.

Another benefit to quantitative easing is that it provides liquidity and a market for securities that are an important function to key sectors of the economy. For example, mortgage-backed securities are an important component to the functioning of capital used to purchase homes. Real estate is an important component to the overall economy. Thus, any stimulation the Fed can provide to the mortgage-back securities market could have benefits to the real estate market.

Open Market Operations

Open market operations are used to lower or raise short-term interest rates and are implemented by the Fed. When the Fed wants to raise interest rates, it goes out into the *open market* and sells some of its treasury bond holdings to buyers in the open market. When these buyers purchase the treasury bonds, they reduce their cash available on deposit at the banks. With less cash in the financial system to lend, banks are more apt to hang on to their cash available to lend unless they can charge a higher rate to borrowers to compensate for the scarcity of available dollars. Conversely, when the Fed wants to lower interest rates, it goes into the open market and buys short-term treasury bonds. The sellers of these bonds now have more cash to deposit into their bank accounts. With more cash in bank accounts, banks have more money to lend. Having more money to lend means the banks are more apt to lend money at lower rates.

The Velocity of Money

The velocity of money is essentially the speed in which cash is allowed to multiply across the entire economic spectrum. In a more formal sense, it is the rate in which money changes hands or turns over in an economy in a given period. Higher velocity means the same quantity of money is used for a greater number of transactions and is related to the demand for money.[11] During a period where consumers are deleveraging (paying down bills), banks are scared to lend, investors are scared to invest, and unemployment is rising, the velocity of money is naturally very low. The concept of money velocity explains why 0 percent interest rates and multiple rounds of quantitative easing have done a poor job of stimulating the economy. This reminds me of the old adage, you can lead a horse to water, but you can't make it drink. You can entice banks to lend and people to spend and borrow, but nothing happens if they refuse to do so.

The Phantom Banking System

There are several markets for debt (as opposed to equity) capital. First, you have traditional banks; if you are a small business and you need a line of credit or a loan, you will typically stop at your local bank on the corner. Second, if you are a large corporation with thousands of employees, you can tap into the bond market. Third, is the derivative market, which is very complex and consists of multiple layers of "securitization." It is the derivative market that is what is known as the phantom banking system. For example, intermediaries raise cash from savers and use this money to buy commercial real estate (or any other cash flow–generating asset). When the pool of cash is exhausted, because all the money has been used to buy cash flow–generating real estate, the intermediary will "flow through" the rental income to the initial providers of this capital. Of course, the intermediary will take in a profit for the "packaging" of this security. The process continues. This is an example of the phantom banking market because it is an untraditional way for people in need of capital to get it. Another widely known synonym for the phantom banking system is securitization. Whether you call it securitization or the phantom banking system, one thing is clear, there can be systemic problems that can be caused as a result of its proliferation. Securitization contributes one huge weakness to today's financial system: The bankers who engage in lending are no longer tied to the risk of the borrower. The lender no longer has the incentive to avoid dangerous risk at all costs because the risk, when cut up into pieces, is quickly shoved out the lender's back door to be packaged with pieces of other risk and to be sold as investment to the unknowing global financial community (Smick 2008, 45).

Perhaps you have heard some of the following terms during the financial crisis of 2008: special investment vehicles (SIVs), mortgage-backed securities (MBSs), collateralized debt obligations (CDOs), commercial mortgage back securities (CMBS), real estate investment trusts (REITs) and other mysterious conduits. These instruments are considered part of the derivatives market because they *derive* their very nature and value from other cash flow instruments. To give you an idea of the significance of the derivatives market, in 2006 the total economic output was valued at $47 trillion. The stock and bond market was valued at $119 trillion. The derivatives market was valued at $473 trillion.

SIVs

SIVs were the main culprit behind the money market debacles that characterized the financial crisis of 2008. You remember the phrase "breaking the buck"? This was where investors were fearful that money markets could be valued at less than $1 per share, which meant that you would lose money. Money markets were supposed to be equivalent to cash. SIVs were purchased in the billions of dollars by money market funds clamoring for yield. The SIVs consisted of subprime mortgage-backed securities. The money raised to purchase these subprime securities came from raising cash from the short-term capital markets in what is known as "borrowing short." You borrow money with repayment in less than a year, but you buy securities that mature much later than a year. In essence, you borrow short and "lend long." The problem with SIVs occurred when short-term investors refused to put up money so that these SIVs could pay off the short-term investors that allowed them to buy the toxic subprime assets to begin with. As a result, a liquidity crisis ensued in this market. With no money to pay back the short-term debt that was coming due, and the rapid deterioration in value of the mortgage backed securities that underlie the SIVs, most bank money markets that invested in these assets were in jeopardy of breaking the buck. How can a money market that is supposed to be a conservative investment ever get away with purchasing longer-dated subprime mortgage assets? This is a great question. The answer is because these SIVs had letters of guarantee backed by the large commercial banks. And because of these guarantees, the rating agencies gave them AAA ratings. With these AAA ratings, money market funds were allowed to purchase the SIVs despite their toxicity. In a financial system that is supposed to provide checks and balances, this was a big disappointment.

MBSs

Mortgage-backed securities (MBSs) are formed by buying mortgages, issuing securities based on the mortgages purchased, and selling those securities to investors who are looking for yield. The interest component of a mortgage payment is paid out to investors while the principle component is a return of the investor's capital. The once famous Ginnae Mae bonds issued by Fannie Mae and Freddie Mac are examples of MBSs.

CDOs

CDOs are basically any type of asset-backed security—a security that has another underlying cash flow–generating asset as its core asset—that is carved up into multiple "tranches" and then issued to investors. For example, a pool of mortgages is grouped together (as in the case of MBS discussed earlier) and is further categorized by its cash flow payments and its principle payments. An investor wanting good yield and not worried about getting their initial capital outlay early will own a tranche of these underlying mortgages that are more subject to prepayments. Other investors, on the other hand, may not want their money prepaid early because of interference with income distribution. In this case, the investor will want a tranche of these mortgages that is less likely to result in mortgage prepayments. A CDO is basically a security that subdivides a pool of cash flow–generating assets into unique qualities that are attractive to different investor preferences.

Question and answer

Question: Does the phantom banking system have anything to do with the Glass-Steagall Act and the subprime mortgage mess?

Answer: Yes. The repeal of Glass-Stegall in 1999 allowed investment banks to act as commercial banks and vice versa. This allowed Wall Street banks to lend money to mortgage borrowers. This provided the fuel for what would ultimately be the subprime mortgage market. Mortgage brokers connected Wall Street banks with customers looking for mortgages to purchase homes. These Wall Street firms would package these mortgages into mortgage-backed securities and sell them to investors. The problem occurred because underwriting standards were nonexistent. These mortgages were called "NINJA" loans because they were issued to people with no income and no jobs. Wall Street did not care because the securities were sold to unsuspecting investors.

Monetizing the Public Debt

Monetizing the public debt occurs when the US treasury issues bonds to fund its operations and the purchaser of these bonds is the Fed. Yes, this is akin to printing money just like the quantitative easing discussed earlier. Monetizing debt is thus a two-step process where the government issues debt to finance its spending and the central bank purchases the debt, leaving the system with an increased supply of base money. Monetization of the public debt is inflationary but can also be used as a tool to help stimulate an economy overburdened by private debt. In essence, this type of monetization is a redistribution of the balance of benefits between debtors and creditors. Creditors are typically debased because of the increase supply of bonds as well as the money supply; creditors are paid back with dollars that are worth less. Debtors gain by paying back their debt in inflated dollars while their nominal interest rates stay static.

Different Types of Credit

It is important to understand the different kinds of credit in the system because they each have different impacts to the economy. First you have consumption credit, which is used to purchase goods such as washing machines, vehicles, furniture, etc. Then, there is production credit, which is used to purchase machinery, buildings, and factories that are used in the manufacture of goods or offering of services. Production credit pays for itself through the profit generated by entrepreneurs who use this credit. Lastly, there is margin credit, which is used to buy financial securities using an existing basket of financial securities as collateral. Let's take a look at how these various forms of credit work with each other.

The middle to end of the 1990s was characterized by fairly stable short-term interest rates. The average thirteen-week treasury bill for this period was right around 5 percent. Thus, there was no need for the Fed to be accommodative or tight in its supply of credit above and beyond what credit was already in the economic and monetary system at that time. In the mid 1990s, the country was in a state of equilibrium where no economic actor benefitted from changing his or her behavior. As a result, this time period is a good starting point for this illustration.

The tech bubble in the late 1990s was spurred by the spectacular advancement in technology and productivity that resulted from the Internet and sophisticated software and hardware that was made possible by companies like Microsoft, Cisco, Oracle, and Intel. This "new era" of technology, or perception thereof, created a giant wave of artificially inflated tech stock prices made possible by massive amounts of margin buying. Buying on margin means using your securities account as collateral for a loan, which is used to buy more securities. This created valuations in stocks that were double their historical average. The end result was a major stock market crash with the NASDAQ bearing the brunt of the calamity. In addition, the massive buildup of tech devices created an oversupply of tech-related gadgets.

The Fed in true Fed form came to the rescue with a liquidity infusion that brought short-term interest rates down to 1 percent by the middle of 2003. Where would this credit end up? Certainly not to build out more technology gadgets since there was already oversupply there. The credit went into residential and commercial real estate. "Build it and they will come," hoped real estate developers. This type of credit is production credit because commercial and residential real estate developers borrowed significant sums of money to build with the intent of reselling or generating cash flow that would be used to pay off their loans. Real estate structures don't just appear. You need the following: wood, concrete, labor, tile, copper, steel, petroleum, and a whole lot of capital. But at this point, there is not enough capital in the system to be able to manufacture and support all this new real estate, so a bidding war ensues for this capital. The demand for these inputs causes input prices to go up.

The demand for inputs, including labor, mortgage services, real estate brokers, and other inputs created a demand of its own; a demand for goods and services that would not have happened prior to the credit expansion. This type of credit is consumption credit. Production credit used to build real estate met the demand for real estate that had been building up in the system before the credit expansion, but in addition, it created its own demand—

through investment in all these inputs. Inflation is at its highest level within the cycle when commodity price inflation peaks and production of products to meet consumer demand rubs up against a fixed base of capital. Commodity inflation goes up faster than consumer price inflation because demand for inputs to build structures and machinery causes an immediate increase in commodity prices while the demand that is generated from this investment occurs slowly. Eventually, the investment in inputs to build more supply stops because entrepreneurs will finally begin to realize that there is enough supply of goods and services. At this point, commodity prices stop going up as rapidly. But the consumption credit—the purchase of cars and washing machines, for example—continues, at least for a while. When this occurs, consumer prices move up faster than commodity prices.

In the case of the recent real estate bubble, when real estate prices in 2006 stopped going up, the party was over. In order for production credit to have a sustained positive effect on the economy, there has to be an assumption that there is enough demand in the system to meet the increased supply. Who in their right mind would invest in more property, plant, and equipment when there is not enough demand to meet their existing stock of property, plant, and equipment? Although the above example is a general summary of what helped create the real estate bubble, it can be applied to any situation where excessive credit is made available. In this case, credit expanded beyond the economy's ability to make productive use of it.

There are certain times that economic polices—such as Keynesian policies after World War II—favor consumption credit (whether the government consumes or the consumer consumes) over production credit. In this case, consumption has to soak up all the excess inventory and capacity that is already in the system. This can take time. As consumption continues, demand rubs up against a limited capacity. At this point, consumer prices start to move up faster than input and commodity prices as higher prices are passed on to consumers. Once capacity utilization gets low, then entrepreneurs will begin to build out additional capacity to make more goods. This process of expanding supply and the capital required in that process causes input and commodity prices to go up. It is at this point in the cycle that inflation is at its highest. In order for economic policies to have a positive effect on consumption there has to be an assurance that people will spend more if given the appropriate incentives.

Question and answer

Question: This whole idea of consumption credit and production credit is interesting. I've never really thought about spending in that way. What implications do you think that has to present day fiscal policy?

Answer: This is an especially crucial issue during an election year. The main issue here has to do with incentives and how taxation plays into that. Let's assume tax credits are provided to businesses for capital investment. Companies will borrow production credit. But what if there is already an excess supply of property, plant, and equipment in the system today? Furthermore, what if the level of consumer demand does not justify a whole lot of investment in new productive capacities? If there is already an excess of supply capacity in the system and consumer spending is not what it used to be, these tax credits may not be effective and may lead to needless inflation and bigger budget deficits.

Question: What about an across-the-board tax cut for everybody?

Answer: I would certainly like that. Daddy can sure use a new pair of shoes. All kidding aside, there is very little debate that our country is running a very high budget deficit. I can see how an across-the-board tax cut would help if consumers use those extra dollars to buy goods and services. However, consumers are deleveraging by paying down debt and increasing their savings. The end result could very well be less revenue for the government, thus larger budget deficits, without a commensurate pickup in economic activity. It is a tough position to be in.

Question: I heard about this guy "Keynes" and how he promoted government spending to help stimulate what you call consumption credit. Why not promote government spending?

Answer: For governments to spend, they need to issue more debt to finance this spending. This is probably not the wisest of ideas at this juncture. This is another tough position to be in.

The Credit Cycle—a Look at 2008 and Beyond

A market similar to the decades following the Great Depression or the period between 1966 and 1982 is very possible given the severe hangover resulting from the overpowered credit expansion that occurred between 2000 and 2007.

The fractional reserve banking system allows for credit to expand given a certain base of deposits. As long as banks are at or above their Fed-mandated reserve requirements, they are free to lend. But at some point the credit starts to run dry as the fractional reserve system starts to run its course. What happens eventually is that credit expands too far relative to the economy's ability to make productive use of it. At this juncture, reckless lending occurs and the financial system begins to show signs of cracking as the economy does not have the productive ability to support principal and interest on this credit. Credit is destroyed, thus bank assets begin to drop in value significantly. Bank confidence in the value of their loans deteriorates so they do not lend. To make matters worse, depositors begin to worry about how much reserve assets the bank has to make good on their deposits. If depositors think that the bank is running out of reserves to make good on their deposits, they will make a mad dash to withdraw their money. Eventually, the bank's reserves run out, and they are insolvent. When asset levels are dropping rapidly, and at the same time depositors are making a run on the bank, it is not long before a bank declares insolvency.

To prevent insolvency from setting in for mass quantities of banks, the Fed and the government must intervene to stop the bloodshed. The Fed intervenes by lowering interest rates and quantitative easing. The process of quantitative easing is known as the Fed expanding its balance sheet. Here, the Fed buys financial assets in the open market to provide liquidity to an otherwise dysfunctional market. For instance, the Fed purchased billions of dollars of mortgage backed securities between 2008 and 2011. The government intervenes by spending to get the economy moving to help support principal and interest on its debt. Since banks keep much of their reserves in the form of government bonds, the government is able to help finance their bailout through Federal Reserve purchases of treasury bonds (monetizing the public debt).

In a financial crisis, if the system can print money and buy assets from banks, thus expanding bank's reserves, then banks can lend again. If the economy could not support the previous round of credit expansion, what makes people think it can support this new phase of credit expansion? The idea is that the new government spending and the newly available credit can spur the economy again. The growth in the economy can now support principal and interest in this newly established credit and some of the old; at least that is what is hoped. Credit availability and spending fuel growth, which leads to more growth and so on, but the implicit assumption is that banks will lend freely (like they did before) and households will be open to leveraging (borrowing) themselves again instead of saving.

When banks don't lend freely and people finally begin to slow their rate of borrowing, the government tries to spend its way out of it by pyramiding its own debt to generate consumption demand. In other words, each time it engages in more and more debt issuance than the time before. We have a situation where bank pyramiding of credit leads to more and more household debt, which is fine when people are able to make more and more money and the economy's growth continues unabated. However, when the systemic growth of credit begins to slow significantly, the economy as whole begins to slow. When this happens, credit destruction occurs (as mentioned before) and the government has to bailout the entire system. Thus, more and more household debt leads to more and more government debt. The only good thing that arises from deleveraging is households will eventually begin to save more, reducing our government's reliance on foreign financing.

This cycle of credit expansion, household debt expansion, and government debt expansion has happened continuously throughout history. The year 1861 through 1879 marked rapid expansion of the money supply due to the Civil War. In addition, 1920 through 1929 when gold was pegged to the pound and the pound appreciation allowed other countries to expand its currency accordingly. And recently, we experienced similar credit expansion from 1981 through 2007. In the 1861 through 1879 scenario, many big companies went bankrupt, but the economy continued to produce in the succeeding ten-year period from

1879 through 1889. The experiences of the Great Depression and the financial collapse of 2008 are fresh in the minds of policy makers and consumers. The system will proceed in a slow and methodical fashion so that the economic and financial pain is not experienced again.

Where does the credit and debt cycle go from here (2010)? The answer depends on the intermediate or long-term course of the market. In the intermediate case, the reflation stemming from increased government spending and quantitative easing will help albeit from very low levels of economic activity. Eventually, however, a few years of growth from a low trough the market will anticipate a higher level of inflation. This anticipation will drive prices higher. The Fed and the government finally realizing that the economy is self-sustaining and feeling that the financial crisis is behind them will begin to take liquidity out of the system to slow the rate of inflation. Not knowing how much liquidity is going to be taken out, the banking system will again be frozen due to the uncertainty of reserve requirements. In the intermediate term, we may see a rise in the market for a period of a couple of years followed by another recession. But the recession should not be as severe as the one before.

In the long run, twenty to thirty years in the future, credit expansion will be subdued leading to a slow growth environment. But this may be the best course for the market. Eventually, the financial crisis will be a distant memory for most and not a memory at all for new entrants to business. There will be plenty of pent-up productivity waiting to be unleashed. There will be plenty of ideas generated over the previous twenty years that need credit to fuel its growth. Then, all over again, we will have another period of massive credit expansion.

Chapter 8

POLITICS—THE BATTLE FOR IDEAS

The political conditions that concern investors the most have to do with the degree of regulation or deregulation, which is based on ideas on how to best handle dislocations and crisis that have occurred throughout history. It is these ideas that determine the policies that dictate the interplay among the state, business, and labor. Investors must understand the power struggle among these entities and which entity is to have the most influence in the years and decades to come.

During times of important economic and social transformations politics take front stage. It is during these times that many investors make rash investment decisions based on their political affiliation. If your own party is in power, things may be assumed to be moving safely enough; but if the opposition is in, then clearly all safety and honor have fled the state.[12] Ultra conservative investors will find a way to rationalize their investment decisions in the wake of liberal policies. Conversely, ultra liberal investors will find a way to rationalize their behavior during times of conservative policy. In October of 2008, during the midst of the financial crisis, a client directed me to sell all his equities because he "did not like the direction the country was going." It was widely expected that President Obama would win by a landslide. When I asked my client how that would affect asset prices, he told me "businesses will no longer have an incentive" and hung up. This client was out of touch with historical precedence as world economies have gone through cycles of increased regulation to deregulation and back again for over two hundred years. I did not tell him that that FDR's first three years in office led to spectacular stock market gains.

Taxation is a sore topic for many people. Increased taxation has recently been associated with the Democratic Party. During the aftermath of the financial crisis of 2008, it was believed by many that President Obama would raise taxes to help cover the tremendous budget shortfall that resulted from the fiscal stimulus and the tax cuts that had been enacted during the eight years prior. November 2009 I attended an economic forum where a Republican panelist said that the only way to create jobs was for the government to stop spending and to cut taxes. Although I generally do not like higher taxes, I wanted to ask how cutting taxes so that consumers can spend more is any different than government spending in creating new jobs. After all, spending is spending no matter who does it. When the government spends money, you know the money will enter the economic system. If the government cuts taxes so citizens can spend more, there is no guarantee that citizens will spend this extra money.

The severe dislocations that occurred in the 1930s gave rise to increased regulation. The severe inflationary and foreign exchange crisis of the 1970s undid many of the institutional regulatory frameworks that existed during the previous several decades. Mark Blyth describes this rotational nature of regulation, deregulation, and back again as embedded liberalism and disembedded liberalism respectively. When referring to the inflation and currency crisis of the 1970s, Blyth indicates that business groups and private interests prevailed to disembed the embedded liberalism that came before it by using a variety of monetarist, inflation control, and other neoclassical ideas away from the Keynesian emphasis on redistribution and growth. Blyth uses the 1930s and 1970s as an example of embedded and disembedded liberalism:

> Just as labor and the state reacted to the collapse of the classical liberal order during the 1930's and 1940's by re-embedding the market, so business reacted against this embedded liberal order during the 1970's and 1980's and sought to "disembed liberalism" once again. In this effort, business and its political allies were quite successful, and by the 1990's a new liberal institutional order had been established in many advanced capitalist states with remarkable similarities to the regime discredited in the 1930's. (Blyth 2002, 6)

When speaking about institutional change, Blythe argues that economic and financial crisis are caused by institutions—the gold standard or welfare state—and thus when crisis occurs these institutions are to blame. To break down these institutions and pave the way for new institutions, the ideas that the former institutions were based on have to be discredited. In this way, new ideas can be used as a political weapon in which to bring about change (39). The delegitimization of these institutions is largely a political matter and thus should be understood.

The first decade of the twenty-first century will go down in history as a lost decade, similar to the 1930s. In addition, the financial crisis of 2008 will go down in history as one of the worst since the Great Depression. It is at this juncture that investors must understand the institutional change that will occur and the political process in which it happens. The deregulation that occurred at the beginning of the 1980s paved the way for significant growth for the next two decades, however, the problems caused by this growth were deeply felt beginning with the Tech Wreck of 2000 and ended with financial collapse of 2008. It is at this juncture that investors can expect an intense degree of political jawboning and increased institutional change. *Institutional changes based on new ideas and the discreditment of old ideas is a time consuming and politically heated process that usually takes years and sometimes decades to complete.* The public anxiety and confusion that accompanies these institutional changes creates volatility and sometimes sharp cyclical reversals in stocks. As a result, investors should pay keen attention to the political landscape in so far as it affects new ideas that can shape the way the state, business, and labor react in this new environment.

Politicians and their allies frequently use the power of ideas to build coalitions to further their own interests at the expense of the opposition. Put simply, economic ideas not only facilitate collective action and radical policy change but are in fact a prerequisite for them. Building upon the notion of ideas as resources, which specify the ends of collective action, it is hypothesized that such ideas also provide agents with the means of achieving those ends (Blyth 2002, 39). For example, the Great Depression has been blamed on ideas of monopolistic competition, lack of sound finance, not enough monopolization, etc. But regardless of the true culprit and despite the sheer magnitude of the depression and the uncertainty it generated, it caught the Republicans, the party of prosperity, by surprise (51). To counter and delegitimize these ideas, new ideas came to the forefront. Ideas based on John Maynard Keynes stabilizing techniques to assure slow and steady growth became dominant in the immediate postwar era and served as the intellectual underpinning of America's version of embedded liberalism until the 1970s (50–51).

For the purposes of investment success, it is important that investors understand the role that ideas have in furthering a political agenda. Ideas carry with them a great deal of emotional baggage. *Taxation, fiscal soundness, health care, inflation, regulation, deregulation, etc., are all weapons that politicians use to stimulate anger and anxiety among the populace to create coalitions to further their own agenda and to put them on top of the power struggle.* Understanding the role of these weapons will help investors look past their own emotions and anxieties and place themselves in a better position to objectively analyze the landscape to help determine the direction of influence among the state, business, and labor. Knowing which of these groups has the most bargaining power on the political stage gives investors insight on what potential changes to expect.

Question and Answer

Question: After the financial collapse of 2008, what structural changes do you see on the horizon?

Answer: The lax banking regulation that perpetuated the financial collapse of 2008 will lead to much more regulation. Liberalism will be embedded again. In fact, we are seeing that now with the Dodd-Frank bill and its promotion of the Volcker rule, which prohibits commercial banks from engaging in proprietary trading and other speculative investing that does not benefit its customers. In addition, lower taxes will give rise to higher taxes.

The twenty-seven years prior to 2007 created many multimillionaires because business conditions were strong, productivity intensely high, and the leap in technological advancement was the strongest it has ever been. The next couple decades will be characterized by redistributing this wealth from those who made it to those who need it. As such, business may be in battle with labor and the state for a long time.

But rather than look at these changes in a vacuum, it is important to have an international perspective. While growth in the United States will slow, growth in the emerging markets, especially China, should be robust. Because many American companies are already so entrenched in foreign markets and because American companies are the five-star standard across the world, American business should still be strong. Although globalization has encountered a temporary setback, the longer-term trajectory for globalization is still positive, thus on balance free market capitalism is still the path of least resistance.

For purposes of profiting in financial markets, don't bet against American blue chips and figure out a way to take advantage of market volatility.

Chapter 9

ECONOMIC PHILOSOPHY

A history of economic thought is important in understanding today's sociopolitical and economic environment because of its effect on ideas and, in turn, how those ideas serve to advance the political interests of those responsible for economic policies that effect all spheres of life. The professional economist is the specialist who is instrumental in designing various measures of government interference of business. He is an expert in the field of economic legislation, which today invariably aims at hindering the market economy (Von Mises 1963, 869). Economic ideas are the biggest political weapons that are used to advance a political agenda. For example, regulation of the business mavericks that are responsible for the destruction of our financial system is an idea. Deregulation that makes it easier for businesses to invest, grow, and expand is an idea. Making home ownership an American dream is an idea. Socialism is an idea. Providing security through entitlement programs is an idea. Providing incentives for innovation is an idea. The list goes on. This is what politics is all about, a battle for ideas that will win with the populace and how to discredit other ideas. However, ideas that win votes may not be ideas that are best for the country as a whole. In this chapter, I cover some ideas of economic philosophy that have shaped generations of American history. Some of these philosophies are like a rotating door, in some environments they work and in others they don't, and when they don't work, these ideas are thrown out and different ideas take their place.

As already discussed in the previous chapter, ideas serve to embed and disembed liberalism, which has been a continuous theme all throughout history. Guy Kawasaki (2004, XI), in describing the yin and yang of business cycles:

> In the microscope phase there's a cry for level-headed thinking, a return to fundamentals, and going back to basics. Experts magnify every detail, line item, and expenditure, and then demand full-blown forecasts, protracted market research, and all-encompassing competitive analysis. In the telescope phase, entrepreneurs bring the future closer. They dream up the next big thing, change the world, and make late-adopters eat their dust. Lots of money is wasted, but some crazy ideas do stick, and the world moves forward. When telescopes work, everyone is an astronomer, and the world is full of stars. When they don't everyone whips out their microscopes and the world is full of flaws.

This shift in mentality is exactly what happens during more difficult times. It is during this cycle of boom to bust that old ideas are thrown out and new ideas are favored. Part of understanding the current environment is deciding when a change from old to new ideas is taking place, who the actors are in making those decisions and what new ideas may implant the old ones. The environment that will define the first quarter of the twenty-first century is one where new ideas and new institutions based on a new or renewed school of economic thought will disembed the old. The greatest works of economists have the potential to provide insights into current economic developments and policy changes (Tsoulfidis 2010, back cover).

In this chapter, I will summarize the basic schools of thought that have shaped or influenced many important historical transitions with the thought that once again these ideas, in whole or in part, will resurface. To add credence to this point,

Newt Gingrich, who was in the running to be the Republican presidential candidate, during an early morning interview on January 5, 2012, on CNBC, was commenting on Adam Smith's economic philosophies. How timely.

This chapter on economic philosophies is merely a summary with the sole intent of providing broad generalizations in philosophical economic thought as opposed to a thesis-like dissertation. Each of the economic philosophies and the people responsible for their advancement that are discussed are not mutually exclusive in their conclusions. There are times when multiple theories are at play at once, but usually one philosophy dominates. Certainly, some of the premises of the more recent schools of economic thought aggregate theories from other philosophies and build from older models. But despite some overlap, each of these theories does have its own unique characteristics. In the following section, I will capture these main ideas.

Economic Philosophies

Mercantilist

One of the earliest forms of comprehensive thought given to economic wealth dated back to Christopher Columbus in the late fifteenth century. Mercantilism was a political movement and an economic theory that advocated the use of state's military power to ensure local markets and supply sources. Mercantile theorists thought international trade could not benefit all countries at the same time. Because money and gold were the only source of riches, there was limited quantity of resources to be shared between countries. Essentially mercantilism advocated countries to export and not import as the former would lead to more wealth creation. Mercantilism was popular during the feudal days of lords and servants. Perhaps when the world runs out of natural resources and the ecosystem begins to deteriorate, mercantilist ideals will once again be popular as countries scramble and raid each other for scarce natural resources.

Classical Economics (Supply Side)

Supply side economics, also known as the labor theory of value, states that prices reflect inputs—labor, commodities, capital— that go into their production. Adam Smith, in his book, *Wealth of Nations*, which was first published in 1776, the same year as the Declaration of Independence, was credited for this labor theory of value. In essence, he posited that the natural price of a commodity was determined by the inputs involved in the manufacture of that commodity. Inputs include land, labor, rent, profits, and anything used in the production process. This theory known as the adding up theory of value, according to which the value of a commodity is determined by the sum of three natural incomes—that is natural wages, natural profit, and natural rents (Tsoulfidis 2010, 28).

Supply side economics base changes in price on changes in the level of competition. For instance if profits are high for businesses, more entities will want to be involved in the production and subsequent sale of the commodity in question. More suppliers will drive the price down. If prices were to drop too low, then some suppliers will no longer find it advantageous to produce and will drop out of the market. This in turn, will cause prices to rise. Supply side economics (classical economics) is a business-centric economic framework. The term *classical economics* has also been used by John Maynard Keynes to include all economists that accept Say's law of markets, which says that "supply creates its own demand" (Tsoulfidis 2010, 134).

In fact, many of President Reagan's policies were based on this modern version of the supply side idea. In his 1980 campaign speeches, Reagan presented his economic proposals as merely a return to the free-enterprise principles that had been in favor before the Great Depression. At the same time he attracted a following from the supply side economics movement, formed in opposition to Keynesian demand-stimulus economics. This movement produced some of the strongest supporters for Reagan's policies during his term in office. The battle between supply side economics and Keynesian economics that occurred in the late '70s and early '80s is a good example of the battle for ideas. A major distinction between classical economics and neoclassical economics (to be discussed later) is the latter assumes that effectual demand determines prices paid for goods and not the inputs that went into the manufacture of them. Where neoclassical economics utilizes traditional supply *and* demand curves to assess equilibrium prices, classical economics does not. Rather, classical economics assumes producers not only supply goods to the market, but these same producers also represent consumption demand using their excess profits to spend on other goods. For example, if you are a pencil manufacturer and your cost to make a pencil is $1, but you sell it for $2, the excess profit of $1 per pencil is used to increase consumption.

In talking about the usefulness of classical economic theory, Lefteris Tsoulfidis (2010, 135) states:

> The classical school of economic thought is not necessarily an approach of the past but finds application also in the present, as this can be judged by the virtue of the fact that in the recent decades an increasing number of economists base their research on the same set of data (or independent variables) as the old classical economists did. In our view, this definition of classical school is still operational and even modern economic problems can be addressed with it.

Neoclassical Economics (Demand Side)

Demand side economics, also known as the marginalist school, asserts that instead of the price of a good or service reflecting labor that had produced it, it reflects its *marginal usefulness* of the last purchase. This means that in equilibrium, peoples' preferences determine prices, including, indirectly the price of labor. While the basis for classical economics rests on labor and other inputs in determining the price of the end product, neoclassical economists use one's *utility* as the major factor in determining prices, hence the name demand side economics—the price paid for a good is dependent on the demand for that good.

Neoclassical economics is the basis in which modern textbooks in economics base their derivation of price. Essentially you have a demand curve, which is a collection of all the individual demand curves into an aggregate schedule of demand that would occur at various prices, and you have a supply curve, which is a function of aggregate total supply from all competitors in the industry. From the intersection of the aggregate demand and supply curves, one can determine the price and the quantity associated with a particular market.

Classical economics, based on the labor theory of value where the values of commodities were dependent upon the labor involved, was widely accepted prior to the midnineteenth century during a time of simplicity and basic subsistence. However, the changes that started to occur during the Industrial Revolution began to outgrow these classical premises in favor of a more sophisticated model of human behavior. Tsouldfidis (2010, 135) points out:

> The idea that the value of commodities was determined by their labor content was too challenging for a system that underwent a structural transformation. Industrial capitalists, up until the middle of the nineteenth century, were directly involved in the production process in the incessant pursuit of expanding profits as a purpose in itself...the growth of corporation and the subsequent concentration and centralization of capital that took place during the depression of 1873 – 1896 changed the structure of the economy as well as the role of the capitalist.

Neoclassical economics was born. This transition in economic theory and thought was necessary to help understand a much more complex social phenomenon. Changes in explanatory theories are a regular occurrence throughout history. These changes occur to be better aligned with conditions prevalent at those times. The understanding of these economic theories and there uses as weapons by politicians is something that needs to be understood to have a sense of what changes may likely occur.

Currently, mainstream economics, which is a combination of neoclassical microeconomic theory with Keynesian macroeconomic theory is the predominate frame of reference when people refer to the study of economics. Neoclassical economics, classical economics, and monetarism (to be discussed later) generally share a distaste for significant government intervention. For neoclassical economics, economics is the study of allocation of resources. In this school of thought, economics is defined as the study that considers human behavior as a relation between scarce means and alternative ends. Moreover, neoclassical economics assumes that all individual actors seek to maximize their own profits as a basis for allocating resources. Usually, neoclassical economists believe that *free markets* bring about the most efficient means of allocating resources.

Keynesian

Keynesian economics is a macro theory based on the twentieth-century British economist, John Maynard Keynes, Keynesian economics argues that private sector decisions sometimes lead to inefficient macroeconomic outcomes and therefore advocates active policy responses by the public sector. It is within mainstream economics that large differences exist between what is acceptable active public sector involvement and what should be left to private free markets.

The academic world that favors the Keynesian view is known as the saltwater schools and consists of schools such as Harvard,

Columbia, and Berkeley. According to saltwater economic theory, the government has an important discretionary role to play in order to actively stabilize the economy over the business cycle.[13]

According to the Keynesian view of the principle of effective demand, governments should spend money on public works that will in turn be used to stimulate demand and ultimately lead to an increase in income and employment. From this increase in income, savings will increase, which will lead to an increase in investment. Investment, in turn, will lead to further increases in income and employment and so on. This process will continue until the natural rate of unemployment is reached.

In much of the parlance of economic theories is the relationship between savings and investment. Neoclassical economics believes the link between savings and investment is through interest rates. The higher the interest rate, the higher the level of savings. Classical economics assumes that whatever the level of savings exactly matches the level of investment. According to Keynes, the equating factor between savings and investment is the level of income; more income means more saving. For Keynes, the independent variable in his analysis is investment expenditures, which determine savings and not the other way around (Tsoulfidis 2010, 249).

Monetarism

The monetarist school of economic thought, that is, the school of economic thought according to which the quantity of money is the utmost important economic variable whose changes affect the behavior of the entire economic system (Tsoulfidis 2010, 301). Milton Friedman through his work at the University of Chicago is widely accepted as the leading theorist and proponent for the monetarist school of thought. However, I would also include Anna Schwartz in there to as a significant figure in the propulsion of the research involved that underlie its premises. The general idea behind monetarism is that an increase in the money supply will naturally lead to an increase in the demand for goods and services, and in turn, prices will rise commensurate to the increase in the supply of money; the opposite is also true—a reduction in the money supply will lead to a reduction in the demand for goods and services. The monetarist school of economic thought also assumed that a free market, unhindered by government intervention, was a necessary prerequisite in the natural function of the economy. Tsoulfidis (320–321) summarizes as follows:

The basic propositions of modern monetarists are the following:

1. Variations in the supply of money are responsible for the variations in nominal income.

2. The market forces are powerful enough to lead the economy to equilibrium except for sudden shocks in money supply. Yet even in this case the economy returns eventually to its initial equilibrium position characterized with natural unemployment.

3. The inverse relationship between inflation and unemployment does not hold in the long run, where the Phillips curve is vertical to the point of natural unemployment

4. Inflation is, always and everywhere, a monetary phenomenon.

Monetarism came into prominence during the stagflation associated with the 1970s. During this time, the driving force behind most major economic philosophies were Keynesian in nature; however, this decade could not explain the Phillips curve, which states that inflation and unemployment are inversely related to each other. This relationship was a basic tenant of Keynesian economics. As such, the credibility of the Keynesian school of thought was in jeopardy, thus opening the doors for monetarism despite the latter's inability to explain the high inflation at that time.

Austrian Economics

Austrian economics focuses less on mathematical algorithms than mainstream economists to explain complex social and economic relationships. Austrians hold that the complexity of human behavior makes mathematical modeling of the evolving market extremely difficult and advocates a *laissez-faire* approach to the economy. Austrian economists focus on motives. Once the goals of the actors and their ideas about the appropriate means for achieving these goals have been established, economic theory, along with other sciences, is brought to bear to trace out effects of these actions in producing complex events and processes of history which are only partially and imperfectly captured in statistical data (Salerno introduction in Rothbard 2005, 10). Austrian economists believe that inflation should be controlled at all costs and that the market should be free from all government interference.

Another distinguishing feature of Austrian economics is its use of history as a means of providing insightful conclusions about present-day problems. Ludwig von Mises in an essay written in 1962 (D. Van Nostrand Company, Inc), "History establishes the fact that men, inspired by definite ideas, made definite judgments of value, chose definite ends, and resorted to definite means in order to attain the ends chosen, and it deals furthermore with the outcome of their actions, the state of affairs the action brought about."[14] According to Joseph Salerno (in introduction Rothbard 2005, 13):

> The subject of history, on the other hand, "is action and the judgments of value directing action toward definite ends." This means that for history, in contrast to economics, actions and value judgments are not ultimate "given" but,

in Mises's words, "are the starting point of a specific mode of reflection, of the specific understanding of the historical sciences of human action." Equipped with the method of "specific understanding," the historian, "when faced with a value judgment and the resulting action…may try to understand how they originated in the mind of the actor."

Marxism

Marxism as a school of economic and social thought is named after Karl Marx (1818–1883). Marx was critical about the detrimental societal effects of capitalism and therefore favored a social system based on equality. Eventually, socialism would give way to a communist stage of history: a classless, stateless system based on common ownership and free access, superabundance, and maximum freedom for individuals to develop their own capacities and talents.

On the theory of competition in a capitalist economy, Marxism postulated that firms under the pursuit of profit as a means in itself would encounter challenges with labor on one hand and capitalists on the other. As a result, firms would hunger for more capital to compete, thus causing labor to be more mechanistic and specialized and drive prices down. Lower prices would cause an expansion of market share and eventually the capital within industries would be concentrated in just the hands of a few. Small firms would merge with the larger ones because of their inability to compete. If there is a grand prediction that has been historically validated, it is Marx's law of increasing concentration and centralization of capital (Tsoulfidis 2010, 122). According to Tsoulfidis (123) when discussing Marx's view of capitalism and the falling rate of profit:

> The realization of the goal of profit maximization entails mechanization of the production process through the introduction of fixed capital. On the one hand, this raises the productivity of labor and profits for the firms

that remain following concentration; on the other hand, however, the increase of fixed capital relative to labor leads to a falling profit rate. Marx noted that the fall in the rate of profit exerts a negative effect on the mass of real profits and, at the same time, a positive effect through the accumulation of capital. So long as the positive effect exceeds the negative, the mass of real profits expands at an increasing rate in a long wave-like pattern. Because new investment is a function of the rate of profit it follows that a falling rate of profit at some point will necessarily slow down the rate of growth of new investment, thereby slowing down the rate of increase in the mass of real profits...there will be a point where the net profit is zero...This is the point of "absolute over-accumulation of capital" that marks the onset of economic crisis...As more and more firms are led into bankruptcies and real wages fall, one can also observe the creation of new institutions, the emergence of new methods of management, and the diffusion of technological change....these processes results in a rising mass of profit and sets the course for the reestablishment of the necessary conditions for another wave of expansion and contraction. Thus, capitalism is both a growth and crisis prone system.

Because Marx's views on socialism have been so pronounced during a time where most of the world was pursuing capitalist ideals, his theories have been completely rejected in any modern discourse on the functioning of economic systems or any policy prescriptions used to fix its problems. However, his analysis and evaluation of economic systems is quite sophisticated and thought provoking and therefore should be judged, no matter how minimally, on his thorough evaluations instead of his conclusions on the proper functioning of a sociopolitical and economic system.

Methods of Study

Because figuring out what motivates people to act is so important in making money, several methods of analysis have emerged. The determination of method may lead to different conclusions; therefore, it is important to know what some of these methods are.

British School

In the British style, international political economy is less wedded to scientific method and more ambitious in its agenda (Cohen 2008, 4). In regard to a less scientific approach, the British school is similar to the Austrian school of economics in terms of studying human behavior. Rather than use complex mathematical formulas that require a supercomputer to figure out, British school advocates prefer common sense and a historical approach to understanding the complex sociopolitical and economic environment. In addition, the British school focuses more on understanding how the world *actually* works rather than theorize how it *should* work.

American School

In the American school, priority is given to scientific methods in what might be called a pure or hard science model. Analysis is based on the twin principles of positivism and empiricism, which hold that knowledge is best accumulated through an appeal to objective observation and systematic testing. Cohen (2008, 40), when discussing the differences between John Galbraith and Paul Samuelson, noted, "Galbraith and his like were drowned out by the clamor of ever-greater numeracy and abstraction in the formulation of economic theory."

Technical analysis

Technical analysis provides investors a graphical representation of historical price movements by looking at the "charts." These charts encompass human psychology, expectations about fundamentals, and expectations about risk. Studying these charts and their historical price patterns can help investors anticipate how current chart formations may lead to other known patterns given their historical precedence. It is widely accepted that financial markets discount future fundamentals. Given this, doesn't it make sense to have a framework with which to analyze the market itself? Proponents of technical analysis argue that the study of price and volume patterns do provide this framework. However, most opponents to technical analysis would point out that historical price movement is no indication of future price movement. In addition, opponents to technical analysis argue that the study of price and volume patterns provide no direct insight to the fundamentals of supply and demand affecting prices.

Fundamental analysis

Fundamental analysis is the detailed study of factors affecting supply and demand for a given market. For example, a fundamental study of Intel's earnings would include an analysis of the company's revenue growth, expense control, discount rate, gross and net profit margins, expansion plans, etc. Proponents of fundamental analysis argue that intense study of the factors affecting supply and demand can give skilled investors "insight" into whether earnings will go up or down, which could provide a precursor to stock price movement. Opponents to fundamental analysis argue that much of the data that is used to forecast fundamental variables is historical data, which is no more powerful, yet much more time consuming, than technical analysis given that technical analysis also uses historical data. Another criticism of fundamental analysis is the subjectivity and sensitivity associated with estimating fundamental variables.

While technical analysis concentrates on the study of market action, fundamental analysis focuses on the economic forces of supply and demand that cause prices to move higher, lower, or stay the same. The fundamentalist studies the cause of market movement, while the technician studies the effects (Murphy 1986, 5). Both schools of thought have strengths and weaknesses.

In my career, I have learned to not take sides on which method of study is better than another or which economic philosophy has more merit than another. My only passion is making money, and the best way to do that is to take the strengths of each philosophy and method and apply it to the situation at hand. Conversely, if you are aware of when each philosophy or method is being used in the improper context by the actors on the political stage, you can save yourself a lot of grief by getting your money out of harm's way.

Freshwater versus Saltwater

The universities that tend toward free markets are known as freshwater schools and are comprised of universities such as the University of Chicago and Carnegie Mellon. "Freshwater economists" often reject the effectiveness of discretionary changes in aggregate public spending as a means to efficiently stabilize business cycles. They emphasize that the government budget constraint is the unavoidable connection between deficits, debt, and inflation.[15] "Saltwater" schools, on the other hand, are so named because they are schools near the coasts that emphasize discretionary changes in economic policy; they are the academic world that favors the Keynesian view and consists of schools such as Harvard, Columbia, and Berkeley. According to saltwater economic theory, the government has an important discretionary role to play in order to actively stabilize the economy over the business cycle.[16] Since one's academic study plays a significant role in the shaping of philosophies, a good place to start in analyzing the actors on the political and economic stage is his place of study.

Influential Economic Philosophers

In the following section, I will summarize the most influential economic philosophers who have been influential in economic thought over the past one hundred years and who have recurred numerous times in my own readings and research regarding economic philosophy.

John Maynard Keynes

- 1883–1946
- Schooled at Cambridge
- Keynesian economics

John Galbraith

- 1908–2006
- Phd, Berkeley taught at Harvard and Princeton
- Keynesian economics

Milton Friedman

- 1912–2006
- Undergraduate at Rutgers, master's at the University of Chicago, and PhD at Columbia
- Monetarism

Ludwig von Mises

- 1881–1973

- Schooled at the University of Vienna
- Austrian economics
- British school

Paul Samuelson

- 1915–2009
- PhD from Harvard; spent entire career teaching at the Massachusetts Institute of Technology
- Keynesian economics
- American School

Friedrich von Hayek

- 1899–1992
- PhD from the University of Vienna; spent most of his academic life at London School of Economists, University of Chicago, and University of Freiburg
- Austrian economics
- British school

Adam Smith

- 1723–1790
- University of Glasgow and University of Oxford
- Famous for "self-interest" and "guided by invisible hand"

Karl Marx

- 1818–1883
- University of Bonn
- Famous for his views on socialism as a means to prevent class warfare.
- Marxism

As can be concluded, there are many different theories, both macro theories and micro theories, about how economies should be ran, how individual decisions are made, and many different methodologies in which to calculate their conclusions. The truth is no one set of ideas works well in all environments. However, for purposes of profiting in financial markets, knowing which ideas will have the most influence on policy makers and the weaknesses that underlie them is a tremendous advantage.

After the Great Depression, US policy was dominated by the Keynesian theory, which had the view that generating consumption demand through deficit spending would eventually lead to a natural low level of employment. These policies worked quite well until the 1970s when an underpinning of Keynes theory, which rested on an inverse relationship between inflation and unemployment, known as the Phillip's Curve, could not be explained. The 1970s was characterized by high inflation and high unemployment. It was during the 1970s that Milton Friedman's theory of monetarism gained in popularity. It was Friedman's premise that inflation is always a monetary phenomenon that became popular. During the early 1980's severe recession, it was obvious that something more was required to kick-start the economy. It was during this time that supply side economics became popular. How timely these policies were. These policies gave way to one of the most spectacular gains in technology, innovation, and productivity the world has ever seen. But these policies are quickly becoming discredited and being hailed as the causes of the financial collapse of 2008, causing us to wonder what economic philosophies will shape the next twenty years.

Question and answer

Question: What economic philosophy do you believe in?

Answer: Just like anything else in life, the business cycle is up and down. When the business cycle is up, everybody is a genius, and when the business cycle is down, there is always somebody to blame and reasons why things aren't working. Policy makers, Democrats, and Republicans all think the same way. When business is doing well, it is because they somehow had something to do with it. When business is not doing well, it is the other party's fault. Because of this mind-set, economic philosophies ebb and flow between one and then the other. There is no one philosophy that will always rule. The key is to know what philosophy will be discredited and what philosophy will take its place.

If I had to choose a side, I would most closely follow the Austrian economic school of thought. I recommend reading anything by Ludwig von Mises or Friedrich von Hayek. The best long-term result will occur when markets are free. I also believe that you have to understand the actors and their motives to know how the sociopolitical and economic environment will change. I believe in learning from history. I believe that you cannot fit the complex relationships between human psychology, human behavior, social interaction, politics, and economics into a few nice mathematical models. These models may work in theory, but in the real world, when we are trying to figure out how things actually work and make money at it, these models are not practical. To quote Ludwig von Mises (Mises 1963, 875) in referring to the teaching of economics, "Students are bewildered; in the courses of the mathematical economists they are fed formulas describing hypothetical states of equilibrium in which there is no longer any action. They easily conclude that these equations are of no use whatever for the comprehension of economic activities." In this sense, I prefer to follow the British school in terms of method of study.

Question and answer

Question: What economic philosophy will prevail for the next ten years?

Answer: The next ten years will be characterized by three philosophies. First, you have Keynesian economics, which our current administration is widely influenced by. Second, I think the concern over inflation will provide a check and balance to money supply growth, which is a monetarist phenomenon. Last, mercantilist policies will have an influence as well. One of mercantilist's main premises is to prefer exports over imports, which is the same as favoring domestic employment over policies that export employment.

Chapter 10

SECULAR TRENDS

Relative Decline of the United States

Throughout history, global hegemonic imperial powers have emerged and declined. Great Britain emerged as the global leader after their defeat of France in the Napoleonic Wars in the early nineteenth century only to surrender that leadership role to the United States a hundred years later. During the middle decades of the seventeenth century, the Dutch Republic was the financial and industrial leader of Europe. Dutch goods outcompeted all others in world markets. The Netherlands superiority in the seventeenth century eventually gave way to Great Britain. Now, it appears that the imperial power of the United States is being compromised by the rising Chinese influence. Because the rise and subsequent decline of world powers has occurred so frequently throughout history, perhaps it is part of the natural evolutionary process of human interaction.

Market forces lead to the reordering of society (domestic or international) into a dynamic core and a dependent periphery. The core is characterized principally by its more advanced levels of technology and economic development; the periphery is, at least initially, dependent on the core as a market for its exports and as a source of productive techniques. In the short term, as the core of a market economy grows, it incorporates into its orbit a larger and larger periphery; in the long term, however, due to the growth process and diffusion of productive technology, new cores tend to form in the periphery and then to become growth centers in their own right (Gilpin 1981, 56–57).

Because the rise and decline of nations have occurred so frequently throughout history and extensive studies have been conducted as to the symptoms and causes of these declines, I will expand further on a framework in which to analyze the current predicament of declining influence for the United States. Declining nation-states experience five internal structural transformations in its relative decline.

Internal changes

First, a country faces structural changes in its economy (Gilpin 1981, 159). As a country matures and draws closer to the top of the "S" curve, the economic cost of maintaining the status quo has a tendency to rise (157). To maintain its dominate position, the imperial power must expend resources on military expansion, finance foreign allies, distribute foreign aid, and other costs associated with maintaining the international economy (156). Rising costs and constant or declining resources eventually leads to a severe financial crisis for the dominant power or powers. The society undergoes an economic climacteric as did Great Britain in the latter part of the nineteenth century, and many believe the United States is experiencing the same thing in the contemporary world (160).

Second, maintaining an efficient and technologically advanced military rises in cost. As a society becomes more affluent, the state has to offer more to soldiers to induce them to join the military. Moreover, the diffusion of military processes and technology to other countries increases, thus causing further expenditures on behalf of the dominate power to stay "one-step-ahead" of foreigners (Gilpin 1981, 162).

Third, a rising affluent class causes lower classes of society to want the same amenities (Gilpin 1981, 162). As this consumption demand increases, so does the tendency for entitlement programs such as Medicare and social security in the contemporary world and bread and circuses in the ancient world (Lewis 1970, 239 as cited in Gilpin 1981, 164). The tendency for the public sector to expand faster than the economy as a whole is known as Wagner's "law of expanding state expenditures" (164).

A fourth internal change facing declining nations is the tendency for the economy to transition from a manufacturing economy to a services economy (Gilpin 1981, 165). Although a service economy can continue to grow through its investment in human capital and knowledge, productivity growth declines relative to an economy based on manufacturing. As a result, imperial powers suffer from a decline in productivity growth relative to its own past and less industrialized manufacturing economies (Rostow 1978, 172 as sited in Gilpin 1981, 165).

The fifth, and probably most important internal change affecting declining dominant powers, is the corrupting influence of affluence. Here, Gilpin (1981, 165) explains how psychological shifts in social values, attitudes, and behaviors tear apart what used to be converging public and private interests. In a growing and expanding environment, public and private interests converge because there is plenty of wealth to go around. However, once economic growth plateaus or declines for an extended period of time, private and public interests begin to diverge; private interests call for continued economic incentives for risk taking in an environment of less opportunity while public interests call for government assistance and subsidies.

> During such periods of decline, conservatives lament the corruption of the moral fiber of society. Their indictments of their contemporaries sound similar themes throughout history: the triumph of individual rights over social responsibility, of debilitating equality over creative liberty,

of easy leisure over hard work, of government bureaucracy over productive enterprise, over loss of will over steadfastness, and so forth. The discerning scholar should be wary of accepting at face value such moralizing. Yet the recurrences of these themes in one declining society after another suggests there is truth…To such a people the idea that the world of their rule and privilege could be otherwise becomes inconceivable…With such a state of mind, a people neither concedes to the just demands of rising challenges nor makes the necessary sacrifices to defend its threatened world. (Gilpin 1981, 166)

Does all this sound familiar? Has the United States become a services industry? Is the cost of maintaining an aging baby boomer population an increasing concern? Is the cost of maintaining wars in Afghanistan and Iraq becoming an ever-increasing proposition? Is there a growing discontent between the affluent who have taken risks and made the right decisions and those who want to be like the affluent without taking risks or making the right decisions? The answer to all of these questions is yes, yes, and yes! But rather than be angry and upset about the maturation of our country and the effects, wouldn't it be easier to accept it as a law of growth and decay that has characterized every dominant state since the beginning of time? The sooner we can come to grips with this fact, the sooner we can start making money.

The question that remains unanswered and will probably remain unanswered for a long time to come is, how long will it take for the United States to lose this spot at number one? The answer to this question depends on how long it will take China to transition from a producer nation to a consumer nation and how long it will take other countries to supplant the United States as the number one innovator of technology and other productivity-enhancing processes and ideas. At some point China will have to rely on its own domestic spending to fuel its growth rather than rely on the rest of the world.

Maybe the seeds have been planted in United States for a system and culture of entitlements without a corresponding incentive for innovation. Maybe the seeds have been planted elsewhere, like China, for a culture of consumerism and a system that promotes innovation. Even if these seeds have been planted, it will take forty to fifty years at least for the United States to be supplanted as the number one economy and military in the world. You can throw all the numbers you want into a machine that extrapolates future trends from historical and current data. But it is never that easy. In the case of the United States, you cannot reverse two hundred years of a system based on capitalism, free markets, competition, winning, American pride, and overall industriousness. China has experienced a lot of discontinuity in the past two hundred years, and their infrastructure is still grounded in state-run enterprises. How can you forecast the timing and the rate in which old cultures are replaced with new ones and the timing and rate in which old business processes, managerial processes, and institutions are replaced with new ones? I don't know when the United States will be replaced at the number spot, but what I do know is that it will take a long time.

I mentioned this in the introduction of this book, but it is worthy of mention again. When it comes to profiting in the stock market, it is important that you invest for the time frame that is important to you. Don't get caught up in trends and evolutions that will take decades to occur.

Question and answer

Question: How does the US debt load play into things?

Answer: This is a good question and one that can easily lead to bad investment decisions as investors allow themselves to be guided by fear. The talk regarding potential sovereign bankruptcies in Greece, Italy, and Spain in early 2012 had many people concerned that the same would happen in the United States. I do not want to make light of our current debt level because we have to get this under control. However, there is much more to the story.

We are used to hearing that we have been a debtor country for a long time. Yes, it is true that the United States has ran current account deficits—we buy more from others than they buy from us—for many decades. And yes, it is true that foreign governments finance our ability to do so. But one thing about this picture that is not widely accepted or understood is that the US dollar has been the reserve currency of the world for just as many decades. This means that foreign governments that are used to running current account surpluses—they sell more to others than they buy from them, i.e., Japan and China—usually recycle these surpluses back into the international global financial markets so their currencies don't strengthen too much because that would hurt their export markets. China and Japan constantly run current account surpluses, thus it is no surprise that they are the two largest purchasers of US treasury bonds. Because of the US dollar's reserve currency status, foreigners are ready and willing to buy US-denominated assets, which typically occur in the form of

US treasury bonds. More treasury bonds means more money for Uncle Sam to spend. It is this reserve currency status that allows the United States to constantly run current account deficits and spend as much as she has without major ramifications to date. This benefit is not afforded to other countries that do not have reserve currency status.

Also, when trying to decipher the meaning of high absolute debt loads, one must also consider the concept of liquidity. In this sense, I mean the ability to raise capital to pay off maturing debt. A liquidity crisis ensues when a country has no demand for its debt and therefore cannot pay off its maturing debt. Because of the US dollar's reserve currency status and its importance in the global financial system, a liquidity crisis is unlikely anytime soon. But some countries that have a much lower level of debt-to-GDP than the United States may be subject to a liquidity crisis if all the sudden the market for their sovereign debt dries up. As such, a high debt-to-GDP ratio, such as the United States, may have a more manageable near-term outlook than others with a lower debt-to-GDP burden.

Another factor that must be considered is the degree to which a country's debt is financed internally or externally. Japan has the highest debt-to-GDP ratio of any industrialized country in the world, but because the majority if her debt is held by citizens of its own country, her high debt load is easier to manage because there is less likelihood that there would be an unwillingness to hold this debt.

Inward focus

During difficult worldwide sociopolitical and economic environments countries become inwardly focused. This means that politicians and policy makers will emphasize measures popular to the home country such as the protection of jobs, enhanced security, and other governmental assistance. The only instances when these measures are not implemented in challenging times are during periods involving a liquidity crisis or hyperinflation when, out of necessity, cutting entitlement programs have to be made for investors to have confidence in the home currency. For example, during 2011 and 2012, Greece was basically teetering on a sovereign bankruptcy because of decades of fiscal imbalance without a corresponding increase in productivity. Because Greece was part of the European Monetary Union, France and Germany were relied upon heavily to provide an adequate bailout. In return for a special financing package to help prevent (or delay) a Greek default, France, Germany, and essentially the rest of the world demanded Greece implement strict austerity measures to reduce social security benefits, unemployment benefits, and other entitlement programs. These austerity measures are obviously unpopular for Greece's domestic economy but were necessary to prevent a liquidity crisis. In this case, Greece chose a domestic recession over a sovereign bankruptcy that would have been much worse in the long run.

Countries, just like human nature, seek security when things get bad. From the perspective of government and policy, this usually takes the form of trade restrictions designed to prevent jobs from flowing out of the country and keeping jobs at home. President Obama, in a speech given on January 25, 2012, stated his desire to sign any bill that provided tax benefits to any company bringing jobs back to the United States. These policies are generally known as *beggar thy neighbor* policies as they serve to export unemployment by emphasizing domestic employment. Every country in the world is guilty of beggar-thy-neighbor policies. Here at home, a prime example is saving General Motors, and in doing so, the government hurt Japanese car manufacturers. Some of these policies include tariffs, quotas, and subsidies. When the government makes loans or subsidies to business, what it does is to tax successful private business in order to support unsuccessful private business (Hazlitt 1979, 47). Since the intensification of the crisis in September 2008, the issue of trade protectionism has received considerable attention in the media, reflecting a rise in protectionist pressures in the world.[17] The years before the financial crisis saw rapid growth in the cross-border activities of banks. According to the Bank for International Settlements, the average year-on-year growth rate for cross-border bank credit to non-banks during the 2000-07 period was a sizzling 15.2 percent; since then cross-border credit has fizzled and looks likely to fall further.[18]

I guess one can say that being inwardly focused is a slowdown of globalization where capital, people, ideas, technology, goods, and services flow seamlessly throughout the world. Whether globalization survives in the twenty-first century will also come down to whether voters are politically accepting of globalizations flaws in light of its tremendous benefits (Smick 2008, 214). Globalization, if allowed to operate under free market principals, will lead to a comparative advantage where each country is allowed to specialize in those areas where they are naturally well endowed or are so efficient in certain productions. Trade in those goods and services occur for other goods and services that are produced more cheaply elsewhere. The flaw of globalization boils down to the destruction of domestic industry in areas where a comparative advantage does not exist. These products and services are imported from international providers. Unfortunately, no country has a comparative advantage in everything.

On the broad international scale, all countries pursuing an inwardly focused trade policy at the same time will lead to less competition, higher prices, higher nominal wages, and slower worldwide growth. Slower worldwide growth and rising structural costs such as, Medicare and social security—will lead to a disproportionate growth where, within and across countries, the income gap will become greater. Greater income gaps cause social unrest within and across countries. Eventually, the international economic system may reach a point of maximum strain where the constant pursuit of economic security and profit rubs up against a fixed set of opportunity.

Question and answer:

Question: Do you think being inwardly focused will help the United States vis-à-vis other countries? After all, a trade war with China can lead to an equally detrimental effect at home.

Answer: I think that depends on who has the most leverage and bargaining power in the global economy. Right now, despite the growing middle class in China, the United States is still the consumer nation in the world, the most productive nation in the world, has the best infrastructure in the world, and has the most highly skilled labor force in the world. As such, we have more comparative advantages in one place than any other country in the world. As a result, a trade war with China, or any other country, would lead to a disproportionate loss of jobs abroad than at home.

Because we are an import oriented consumer nation and China is an export oriented producer nation, they stand to lose much more if for some reason they decided to create import restrictions on products made in the US. They don't buy much from us anyway. And, to disallow exports to the US would create job losses in China as their economy is based on exports. But this would certainly not preclude a situation where stupid trade policy on our part could result in trade retaliations on many fronts including countries such as Japan, Germany, Brazil, etc. China certainly has leverage over many countries that may be an important market for US goods. Who is to say they will not engage in "behind the scenes" negotiations that could hurt us? Of course, there will come a time where we won't have most of the bargaining chips in our corner, and when that time comes, hopefully we will have friends—powerful friends.

Question and answer

Question: Do you think we are in the midst of a reversal of globalization and a reversion back to the inwardly focused world economy that characterized most of the rest of the world after WWII?

Answer: No, I think we have experienced only a temporary setback. I think the crashing down of the Berlin wall in 1989 and the collapse of the former Soviet Union in 1991 is symbolic of a new world order that is based on capitalism and free markets. But globalization will be met with domestic challenges, not just here, but abroad as well.

Higher interest rates

Interest rates are essentially the price you pay for credit and are closely related to the supply of money. Just like anything else, this price—interest rates—is affected by supply *and* demand. But what makes interest rates unique is they are "anchored" by treasury rates and the rate that banks charge each other called the Fed funds rate. The Fed funds rate is the short-term interest rate that is controlled by the Federal Reserve's open market policies and is the rate that moves up and down when the Fed raises or lowers interest rates respectively. All markets for credit, whether it is the corporate market, municipal market, or the consumer market for mortgages ebbs and flows with the movement in treasury yields and the Fed funds rate.

Supply of credit

When banks have a lot of cash and there are a lot of savers, interest rates, all else equal, stay low. This means that the supply of cash and credit is plentiful. When credit providers have a lot of cash to loan out *and they feel good about getting paid back*, they will try to get rid of it as soon as possible and to entice people to borrow, they will offer low rates. On a broader international scale, when foreign countries that run large surpluses in their balance of payments want to hold the "reserve" currency of the world—the US dollar—they will buy treasury bonds. All else equal, this supply of credit (or demand for bonds) will drive interest rates down.

Demand for credit

When businesses see great opportunities for profit or new markets to enter, they will demand credit. This demand typically takes the form of bonds or fixed income debentures. When bonds are issued to investors (savers) the supply of bonds go up (the demand for credit goes up) and, all else equal, interest rates go up. When the government needs to borrow additional sums of money to finance its expenditures, they issue bonds and the increase in the supply of bonds (or supply of debt) drives interest rates up. Similarly, when consumers demand credit, interest rates go up.

Supply and demand for credit

Now let's combine the supply and demand for credit. There is a difference between the availability of money and credit and the actual issuance of credit to the end user. The monetary system in 2012 can be characterized by having a lot of supply of cash, and therefore credit. This is due to multiple rounds of quantitative easing. This is why interest rates are so low. Banks have so much cash on reserve that they should be willing to lend it out at low interest rates. Moreover, with the fallout of the euro, surplus countries are demanding treasury bonds, which further depresses interest rates.

However, banks are not willing to depart from their supply of money because the fear of not getting paid back and the uncertainty with regard to future reserve requirements. What cash they are willing to depart with they will want higher rates to justify the risk emanating from a mediocre at best economic environment. Meanwhile, the government is demanding significant sums of capital in light of a reduction in tax revenue. These two phenomena alone are justification that rates should be higher than they are. There is disequilibrium between the economic reality and the availability of credit. The economic reality would justify higher rates but the availability of capital is keeping rates low. Sooner or later the economic reality and the market for money and credit will once again become synchronized, despite any attempt by the Fed to prevent this alignment. *The fundamentals always win in the long run but can be distorted in the short and intermediate terms.*

The relative decline of the United States—and therefore, the desire to buy or hold US-denominated debt—together with the costs associated with maintaining an aging population and an economic reality that will cause the providers of capital to be diligent in their lending will all cause rates to be higher in the long run. However, the aging baby boomer population and their increased savings will help temper this rise.

Question and answer:

Question: I know you said that interest rates are likely to go up over the next few decades, and that makes sense. But interest rates have been low for a long time, and even if they double or triple from here, they will still be low. Do you feel that the low interest rates are actually hurting the economy because people are not making anything on their deposits?

Answer: Interest rates are very low, and people who rely on interest on their investments aren't making much. But the question is do the extraordinary low rates have an overall adverse effect on the economy? Rates are low because there is a lot of cash in the financial system and there are a lot of people saving money. When rates are low, companies will borrow money to expand, entrepreneurs will borrow money to start businesses, and consumers will borrow money to buy things. This "easy credit" situation is supposed to be good for the economy. However, bank credit to consumers and small businesses have been contracting for the past couple years. Banks are well capitalized, and one would think that they would be more open to lending money, but they haven't been. Companies with access to the capital markets are raising a lot of debt capital, but there seems to be a trend toward using this cash for acquisitions and stock buybacks than actually large scale investments. The ultralow interest rates have had an adverse effect on the economy up to this point. However, once banks start to feel more confident about the real estate market and overall business conditions, then they will start lending again. When this happens, the low interest rates will be a good thing for the economy because the pent-up demand for consumer and small business credit will finally be met.

Question and answer:

Question: The Fed has repeatedly said that they are going to keep rates low until 2014. Does that contradict your prediction of higher rates?

Answer: No. We are talking about long term secular trends that will shape the next twenty years. Another thing to keep in mind is the Fed only controls the short term interest rate. It is possible that short term interest rates stay low while the longer term interest rates rise. But, despite what the Fed says about what they plan to do with short term interest rates, they are not mandated to keep their word. Going back to chapter 9 on economic philosophy you have to understand the motivation of the people making these policy decisions. The Fed made their announcement to keep rates low during a time when the European credit markets were falling apart due to problems in Greece, Spain, Italy, and Portugal. Ben Bernanke's motivation at that time was to calm worldwide markets to prevent what could have resulted in a catastrophic spread of a credit crisis. If inflation in the United States spreads faster than what is comfortable for the Federal Reserve and it does so before 2014, they will have no hesitation to raise short term interest rates.

Deleveraging

There is no controversy about the high level of household and government debt. The United States is rubbing up against a debt-to-GDP ratio of near 100 percent while household mortgage delinquencies reached a record high in 2009. Consumers' savings rates have been on an upward trajectory slope since 2008. The fact is plain and simple, that the US government and citizens of its government can no longer continue the pace of spending that characterized the previous fifty years. This doesn't mean every ounce of income is going to be saved, but the rate of spending will have to slow dramatically. The money that would otherwise be made available for consumption will be diverted to paying down debt and saving. The end result will be a much-needed process of balance sheet repair, but at the expense of economic growth. This is not to say that the United States will not grow economically; we just won't grow as fast as what we have become accustomed to.

Question and answer:

Question: I keep hearing about something called the paradox of thrift. Can you tell me more about that and tell me your thoughts on it?

Answer: The paradox of thrift was popularized by John Maynard Keynes and basically states that savings in the economy does damage because people are not spending money. According to Keynes, the level of income determines the level of savings. I would say that the whole consumer mentality behind deleveraging—paying down debt—also applies to savings. When people pay down debt, they are also inclined to save. I think we are going to encounter a significant period of time where people are going to be paying down their debt and saving their money, which means less money for consumption than what we were accustomed to between 1981 and 2007. An era of deleveraging and increased savings is an equilibrium-changing event that will happen slowly. The business and corporate community will adjust to this reduced demand by reducing supply. As long as the free market does a good job adjusting to this reduced demand, a new albeit lower, equilibrium will be in place. The stock market will adjust accordingly. As long as stock market valuations stay contained within a nice respectable level, you can still make money in stocks.

Baby boomers

Baby boomers are the single largest segment of the population in the United States today. This generation consists of those people born between 1945 and 1965, which, as of 2012, makes them between the ages of forty-seven and sixty-seven years old. In the United States, 13 percent of the population is over the age of sixty-five compared with 8 percent in China and 5 percent in India. The explosion of children born after the war in the United States not coincidentally came at roughly the same time that Fannie Mae was formed in 1938 as part of President Roosevelt's New Deal. This emphasis on home ownership and family values helped create a generation that we know of today as the baby boomer generation. But the United States is not alone in this aging population. Japan has 22 percent of its population over the age of sixty-five. Europe's population over the age of sixty-five is somewhere between that of the United States and Japan. The baby boomer population will have several effects on the sociopolitical and economic environment.

Effect on fiscal policy

Supporting the entitlement programs such as social security, Medicare, and Medicaid for the baby boomer population is going to be a tall order for most of the developed world. Over the next twenty-five years our fiscal budget will have to address the increased costs and the reduced productivity—and therefore reduced tax revenues—of the baby boomers as they age and begin to retire. These increased expenditures will crowd out expenditures that could have gone elsewhere for more productive endeavors.

Effect on savings

To a certain extent, the increased costs of entitlement programs for baby boomers will be financed by baby boomers. Their increased savings rates and movement toward fixed income away from equities, particularly in higher interest rate environments, will help fund social security, Medicare, and Medicaid. The higher interest costs associated with the federal debt is something that will have to be worked out over a very long period of time.

The net effect

The net effect of the aging of the baby boomers both here and abroad will result in a much higher expense structure that governments are going to have to support with a much more limited revenue base. Interest rates will go up. More money diverted to the health care system will naturally cause medical care costs to go up for everybody. The good thing is a lot of the baby boomer savings will be diverted to purchasing the bonds issued to pay for these higher costs. This will result in a reduction in interest rates, but the long-term trajectory of interest rates will still be higher as supply will more than soak up demand. In general, the demand for equities will drop and the demand for fixed income instruments will rise as baby boomers rebalance their portfolios. This will cause some headwinds that the general stock market will have to overcome.

China—the eight-thousand-pound elephant

Throughout history there have been many stories that have flat-out fooled investors into thinking certain countries or regions of the world were going to be the next economic powerhouse. David Smick (2008, 94) summarizes:

> In the late nineteenth century, Europe's most important geostrategists were debating which country would be the next great world power by 1920. In some circles the top choices, believe it or not, were the United States and Argentina, as both nations enjoyed abundant natural

resources. Most British elites who engaged in this debate picked the United States, but a number of Continental experts opted for Argentina as the next great world power, emphasizing its strong tradition of European influence and lack of racial problems that existed in the United States… More predictions: Several years ago, a senior Japanese official dropped by my office in Washington, mostly to talk about China. He produced a copy of *Foreign Affairs* article written in 1957, which argued that the Soviet economy, at the time growing officially faster than the U.S. economy, would become the dominant economic force by the mid-1970s. Later in the 1970s, the conventional view was that Germany would globally dominate; in the 1980s, it was Japan that would run the world. So much for conventional wisdom.

There are many reasons why a country may fail to be a world economic power just like there are many reasons why a country may achieve such status for extended periods of time. In the case of the latter, maybe it has something to do with being at the right place at the right time and doing the right things, which in some respects has to do with pure luck. But whatever the specific case, there are some common elements as to how countries become powerful—although specific paths differ—and why they can stay that way for generations. The three most recent examples include the United States in the twentieth and at least the first part of the twenty-first century, Great Britain in the latter half of the eighteenth century and most of the nineteenth century, and the Netherlands in the seventeenth and eighteenth centuries. Some common elements of these countries include origins based on free markets (or less socialist than other countries, depending on how you want to look at it); productivity; balance of expenditures between defense, consumption, and investment; national unity; no war reparations; and an industrious population. Wealth is the basis for military power; to protect wealth, military power is necessary.[19] To sustain the status of world power post–Industrial Revolution, the opposite is not true that military power is the basis for wealth. The former Soviet Union learned this lesson the hard way as their dominance in the sixties and seventies was based on military might while their underlying economic infrastructure was state based and very weak. A state based centrally controlled economy does not work if the goal is to create strong infrastructures and institutions that can be used as the foundation for social and technological progress.

China has many of the characteristics necessary to be the next world power, thus the ability to garner significant leverage in the international political economy; however, it will take much longer than many people think for this transition to occur. Many believe that this claim in the making is something new. It is not. China has been there before. According to Vaclav Smil (2008, 129):

> Historians of dynastic China would say that *return* would be a more accurate description than *rise*. For about two millennia China was the preindustrial world's largest economy. (Maddison 2001) credited it with some three-quarters of the global economic output at the beginning of the Common Era, two-thirds by the year 1000, and still nearly 60% by 1820. There is little doubt that under Qianlong (1736–1795), the longest reigning of all Qing dynasty emperors, it was on average the more prosperous in per capita terms than England or France (Pomeranz 2001).

I don't think that one should underestimate the effect of China's once economic superiority in their transition to being the world's next top power. They have been there before. For the past 150 years, China has taken two steps forward and one step back in their quest to achieve what they believe is inherently their rightful spot at number one. China, under Mao Zedong's communist regime, until his death in 1976, set the country back fifty years. Before Mao Zedong, China was not a communistic country. By the end of 1979, Deng Xiaoping began to steer the country toward economic pragmatism and reintegration into the world economy. China's one child policy that started in 1978 was meant to build a generation of workers that were industrialists known as "little emperors." The Chinese state enforced a rapid fertility transition designed to cultivate a generation of "high-quality" people with resources and ambition to join the global elite.[20]

China's growing middle class is going to supply the world, as well as their domestic economy, with the type of world-altering consumption demand capable of a positive equilibrium change on a worldwide international scale. The Chinese middle class is already larger than the entire population of the United States. In fifteen years, the Chinese middle class will reach eight hundred million. China has changed, and will continue to change, the dynamics of the world we live in and have a huge impact on everything our life, our jobs, our economy, and the world.[21] As a result of this expectation, foreign domestic investment in China has been staggering. Since the mid-1980s, China has been receiving a rising influx of foreign direct investment, with the 2005 total surpassing $60 billion, compared to $4 billion invested by foreigners in India's economy (Smil 2008, 130).

The one concern I have about China's future dominance in the world economy is its productivity. Efficiency, productivity, and technological dominance all characterized the Netherlands, Great Britain, and the United States during their respective reigns. Whether China achieves such status in productivity will be determined by the speed in which they eliminate inefficient state-ran enterprises and promotes competition within its domestic borders.

Chapter 11

FUNDAMENTALS OF STOCK VALUATION

A careful evaluation of the sociopolitical and economic environment can provide valuable insight into the basic variables that ultimately affect how stocks are valued. This chapter discusses two primary ways stock are valued—discounted cash flow and multiple analysis.

Discounted cash flow

The easiest way for me to illustrate how the various macro environmental factors affect stock market valuation is through a very simplified model of discounted cash flow analysis. The factors are best illustrated using the following discounted cash flow mathematical relationship:

Stock market value = [Free cash flow / (r − g)]

Free cash flow is a company's actual cash flow from operations less any capital expenditures required to sustain its long-term competitive position. Holding the other two variables equal, any factor that increases free cash flow will increase stock valuation. The r in the above relationship represents a company's risk. As can be extrapolated from this relationship, the higher the risk, all else equal, the larger the denominator, which results in a lower stock market value. The concept that more risk results in lower stock market values is an important concept to understand because most of the volatility in the stock market results from real or perceived risks. The *g* in this equation is the growth in earnings. Holding the other two variables constant, more growth results in a smaller denominator, which causes the stock market to go up.

For the S&P 500, the growth in free cash flow and dividend payout increased by 20 percent from January 2011 to January 2012, however the market was virtually unchanged. In addition, growth in earnings had increased 10 percent over the same time period. How could this be? It was because the *r* (the risk factor in the above equation) had gone up due to the problems in Europe. The net result was a balance of all components of the equation. Any macroeconomic factor that increases the growth in corporate earnings causes the stock market to go up. In reality, there can be literally dozens of extremely difficult to predict factors that affect each of the three variables—free cash flow, risk, and earnings growth. Despite these difficulties, having a framework for understanding stock market valuation is a valuable analytical tool.

Holding risk and earnings growth constant, an increase in free cash flow will result in higher stock values. Sometimes analysts prefer to use a company's dividend in place of free cash flow, in which case the higher the dividend payout, all else equal, results in higher stock values. Cash cow companies that increase their dividend payout, without sacrificing earnings growth, should see an increase in their stock price. The same can be said about the stock market as a whole. However, this is often symbolic of a slow growth economic environment because companies would usually prefer to invest in projects that will increase earnings than paying out higher dividends, which are harder to reverse. If companies don't see that there is enough demand to justify new investment, they will usually resort to higher dividend payout rates or just hoard cash.

Risk is associated with any kind of default, banking panic, or any form of derivative fallout. Because these risks are the most severe for an economy, the political will to provide a backstop to prevent a panic is usually pretty high. This is why risk-based corrections don't last that long.

A reduction in earnings growth almost always occurs in a general recession. Earnings growth is sensitive to the economic cycle. Free cash flow and dividend payouts usually do not drop in a plain-vanilla recession unless the recession lasts significantly longer than the average eleven months. This is because free cash flow and dividend payouts can be supported with strong balance sheets for long periods of time, whereas a reduction in earnings growth hits the income statement first.

The worst stock market declines hit all three of the components—free cash flow or dividend payout, risk, and growth in earnings. The financial collapse of 2008, which resulted in a recession that lasted eighteen months, is a good example of what can happen when all three components of the stock valuation model are adversely affected at the same time.

Multiple Analysis

A less scientific method of stock market valuation is to take the latest earnings per share and attach a multiple to it. For example, say the aggregated earnings per share for every company in the S&P 500 is $96 and let's say you apply a multiple of 12 to these earnings, then the estimated value is 1,152. Similarly, if the S&P 500 is trading at 1,152 and the most recent aggregated earnings for this index is $96, then index is said to be trading at "a multiple of 12." If the historical earnings multiple for the S&P 500 is 16, then the market is said to be "cheap." Similar to the simplified discounted cash flow model discussed earlier, multiples are driven by perceptions of risk and growth. A market with more risk typically trades at a lower multiple while and market with less risk trades at a higher multiple. A market with more growth typically has a higher multiple (unless there is a lot of inherent risk) and a market with less growth typically has a smaller multiple.

Part 3
Understanding Market Behavior

Strategy and
Discipline

Understanding
your goals and
objectives

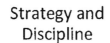

*Understanding
market
behavior*

Understanding
the current
macro
environment

Chapter 12

FIT

Part 3 of this book discusses the nuances of the market that contribute to its often peculiar behavior. *Understand this peculiar behavior, and you will begin to feel the gap between this behavior and the sociopolitical and economic environment begin to close.* Before we go any further, it is worthwhile to explore how Part 2 on Understanding the Environment and Part 3 on Understanding Market Behavior fit together. In sum, a broad understanding of the sociopolitical and economic conditions that define the time period under analysis, and an understanding of market behavior, together will provide investors with a sense of where the economy is within the business cycle and therefore the direction of corporate profits and primary market direction:

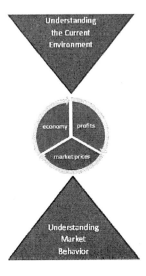

It is a known fact that the market "leads" the economy. Market prices will have a sustainable rise before the economy turns the corner from recession to expansion. Similarly, the market will experience a sustainable period of decline before the market enters into a recession. As such, the market is said to "discount" future changes in economic activity. If this is true, then shouldn't there be some kind of analytical framework in which to analyze the market itself to have a sense of where the economy is going? Part 3 of this book, Understanding Market Behavior, establishes a framework for analyzing market behavior in order to draw conclusions on what this behavior may be saying about the status of the economy. You can write volumes on each of the concepts and methods discussed in chapters 13 through 18. There are plenty of books written on technical analysis, investor and market psychology, cycles, fundamental market variables, and rates of change. However, it is better to know the general ideas and the more important concepts within each field and then combine them into an analytical framework. Having a sense of where the economy is will then lead us down the path of the direction of corporate profits and future primary direction of stock prices.

Before I go further into market behavior, I want to provide an example of how I combine an understanding of the current macro environment with knowledge of market behavior to arrive at a tactical investment strategy. Here is an analysis sent to select clients in January 2012.

Example
Understanding the Environment

Housing is showing significant improvement. Recently we've had a rise in pending home sales, new home sales increased for the third straight month, total inventories dropped again continuing their four-month decline, the lowest level in two years. Housing is important because a bottom here will be a *big* confidence booster for many important segments of the market, including banking. Distressed sales account for 29 percent of the market versus 34 percent a year ago. I feel housing is an important component at this stage of the business cycle because without an improvement here, bank loans will stay at the banks. Fortunately, banks have been increasing their loan volumes as evidenced by a net increase in aggregate bank lending over the quarter. Increasing bank loans and a housing market that is stabilizing should feed on itself and be a powerful source for economic growth in the months to come.

Assuming Europe can kick their woes down the road a few more years, I do not see anything on the horizon that can cause a significant drop in *equilibrium*. The Fed has committed to keeping short-term rates low through 2012, and taxes will not go up in an election year.

Consumers have been *deleveraging* for quite some time now; thus their balance sheets are beginning to heal. This should pave the way for more spending. If longer-term rates begin to rise, investors and consumers may jump on the real estate bandwagon and start buying homes out of fear that rates will move higher.

The environment looks good for 2012, but the recovery may be one of those "be careful what you wish for" events because inflation may become a reality. In addition, August of 2012 will mark the third year since the recession was declared over in August of 2009; maybe a recovery that is getting long in the tooth. Given the devastation of the financial collapse of 2008, the system is prone and sensitive to a "shock."

Understanding Market Behavior

The market's historical tendencies (using month-end data unless otherwise noted): Typically primary bull markets last an average of fifty-eight months with a median of thirty-four months. March 9, 2012, will mark thirty-six months. The average gain in a primary bull market is 209 percent while the median gain is 77 percent. The DJIA return at the end of 2011 was 74 percent. From a *median* standpoint, we are very close to historical tendencies. But from an *average* standpoint, we can continue stronger and longer.

Market and investor psychology: All throughout this primary bull market, investors have not been optimistic and rightfully so due to what they had gone through the previous few years. The highest reading of bull optimists from March 2009 to the end of 2012 was 51 percent according to data from AAII. Also, corporate bond inflows in November were huge. This could be caused by low rates everywhere else or an aversion toward equities. You want to interpret the lack of optimism from the retail public as a positive sign for the market.

Cycles: Election years are typically the second best year of the four-year presidential cycle. The first five trading days of January have a record of thirteen wins and only two losses in election years. If the first five days are positive in election years, so is the market for the rest of the year. Most gains in presidential years occur in the last seven months of the year. Interest rates have a tendency to rise in the first six months of the year. April marks the end of the best six months trading pattern, which occurs November through April. If the DJIA breaks below the low for the month of December in the first quarter of 2012 the market could be in for a very volatile year.

Technical analysis: Looking at the three-year *weekly* chart on the DJIA, which is the first thing I usually do, I see a lot of resistance at the recent high of 12,800 as it has approached that level twice since it initially touched in April 2011. I also see a fair amount of support at 11,000 and even more support at 10,500. Unfortunately, those levels are greater than 10 percent away.

There has been no notable consistency where the market has closed at or near the low for the week. This is a positive sign as the most important period of time for the market is at the end of the trading day, week, or month.

On a weekly three-year basis, there is no negative divergence between price and momentum. The market has retraced *up* more than 62 percent (important Fibonacci retracement level) of the drop between April's high to September's low. This suggests that the DJIA may again approach the 12,800 for a complete retracement.

Looking at the fifteen-year monthly chart on the DJIA as the second thing I look at to obtain a longer-term view, I see that each of the last three months of 2011 have ended on a positive note. The October month's range of returns, with the ending value much higher than the starting value, "engulfed" the September month. This means the low in October dropped below the low in September but closed the month higher than the start of September. This is called a bullish engulfing pattern (to be discussed in chapter 16) and is a good sign.

One technical concern I have, however, is the weakness in the number of stocks trading above their twenty-six-week moving average. This suggests that the market is being propelled by fewer and fewer stocks. A close look at this indicator in the first quarter is warranted.

Another concern I have is the fact that for the hundred-day and two-hundred-day periods, the defensive sectors—healthcare, utilities, and consumer staples—have done significantly better than other economically cyclical sectors. However, this could also be a result of the ridiculously low interest rates.

Fundamentals: Valuations all across the board are good except for domestic mid cap and small cap stocks. Consumer confidence dropped a lot in August and September but has rebounded sharply in Q4, bringing the reading up to the average. Industrial Production is flat and has been for the past three years. Interest rates are definitely bottoming. The yield curve has been flattening due to the long end of the curve coming down quite a bit.

Using Sam Stovall's framework (see chapter 15) for assessing the business cycle suggests that a full recovery is expected for 2012.

High yield credit spreads at 6.4 percent are up from the cycle low of 4 percent but, significantly, below the early 2009 levels. Perception of risk has increased from three months ago, but not up to alarming levels.

Putting It All Together

Technicals are the biggest negative as sector rotation has definitely favored the defensive sectors the last seven months of 2011. Maybe this could be a result of rates dropping so low and investors clamming for yield. Also, the percentage of stocks trading above their twenty-six-week moving average is also a bad sign. But these are balanced with other positive technicals.

Not sure if this primary market will veer toward its historical average tendency or median tendency. Average tendency would suggest the market strength can continue for many more months. Median tendency would suggest the market will soon begin a primary bear market.

But everything else remains positive:

- Investor psychology is still not bullish, which is optimistic for stocks
- Environment and fundamentals look positive
- Cyclically, election years are relatively good. Pay attention to January's first five trading days.

Chapter 13

THE MARKET'S
HISTORICAL TENDENCIES

Knowledge of historical market averages is a great starting point in which to analyze the market. How long does the average primary bull or bear market last? What is the average performance of a bull or bear market? During a bull or bear market, on average, how long does it take before we have a countercyclical correction or period of consolidation? When a countercyclical correction does take place, on average, how long does it take and how deep? Having some knowledge of market averages is a powerful tool; however, using historical averages should only be used in conjunction with other analytical tools. Historical averages should be adjusted—up or down—depending on the situation and many other considerations.

Bull and *bear* markets are traditionally defined as markets that move up or down respectively by 20 percent or more. My frustration with truncating these terms at their percentage gain or loss is that the definition does not provide a *time* component. For example, there are many instances of market drops or rises that have lasted very short periods of time. These sharp movements are hard to predict and time. Black Monday, October 19, 1987, is a good example. August and September of 2011 is another good example. During these declines, the market had a full recovery three months later. Reacting to these sharp moves can be very frustrating because it usually results in selling at the bottom. The most important trends to be in front of are the ones that result in large percentage moves *and* have long durations. To my knowledge, there is no compilation of research done on historical stock market data that combines price data with time data.

As such, I have done the research myself using monthly data points from the DJIA dating back to 1900. I define bull markets that result in a minimum of a 20 percent increase *and* have a duration of at least twelve months a *primary* bull market. Similarly, I define bear markets that result in a minimum of a 20 percent decline *and* have duration of at least twelve months a *primary* bear market. I define *intermediate* market moves as those moves within primary trends that go counter to the primary trend and only last two to seven months (give or take). I chose to use data going as far back to 1900 because I wanted to encompass many different sociopolitical and economic times and include multiple financial collapses. Financial collapses occurred after the San Francisco earthquake in 1906, the Great Depression of 1929, and financial collapse of 2008. Including more data points make the conclusions more meaningful. I will share with you some conclusions of my research using month end data for the DJIA:

- There have been sixteen primary bull markets since 1900
- There have been seventeen primary bear markets since 1900
- The average return for the sixteen primary bull markets is 208 percent
- The average duration for the sixteen primary bull markets is fifty-eight months
- The median return for the sixteen primary bull markets is 77 percent
- The median duration for the sixteen primary bull markets is thirty-four months

- The average return for the seventeen primary bear markets is -37 percent
- The average duration for the seventeen primary bear markets is twenty-two months
- The median return for the seventeen primary bear markets is -36 percent.
- The median duration for the seventeen primary bear markets is twenty-one months

The key takeaways from the above data are the following:

- Primary bear markets are more defined than primary bull markets. The average decline for a primary bear market is -37 percent while the median is -36 percent. The average duration of a primary bear market is twenty-two months while the median is twenty-one months.
- Primary bull markets have a strong bias to upside returns. The average rise for a primary bull market is 208 percent while the median is 77 percent.
- It is much more difficult to predict when a primary bull market will end than it is to predict when a primary bear market will end.
- Loss aversion is stronger than missing out on returns. As such, investors are less likely to want to buy when the market is dropping and more likely to sell and take gains (out of fear their gains will dissipate) while the market continues to drift higher and higher.

The primary bear market that encompassed the financial collapse of 2008 lasted eighteen months from October 2007 through March of 2009 and resulted in a decline of -49 percent. The decline was larger than the average decline but ended sooner than the average length of time for a primary bear market. It is not common that a primary bear market include a recession, financial collapse, and asset bubble (residential real estate) occurring all at once, which was the case in 2008. The last instance of such devastation was during the Great Depression. With many comparisons between the Great Depression and the financial collapse of 2008, policy makers acted much more swiftly, decisively, and aggressively than they did during the former event. For example, in 1930 Congress passed the Smoot-Hawley tariff legislation, which was a tax on imported goods. Foreign nations retaliated with similar policies of their own; foreign trade came to a screeching halt. In addition, in 1931 the Fed increased interest rates by two hundred basis points, and in 1932 marginal income tax rates were raised. During the financial collapse of 2008, not only were short-term rates dropped to zero, quantitative easing occurred through multiple rounds of asset purchases. These more aggressive policy actions were the first clues that the primary bear market of 2008 would end sooner than the average.

I isolated each primary bull and bear market and magnified it to understand how each of these primary moves behaved. Obviously, the market does not move up or down in a straight line. At some point within its primary advance or primary decline, the market will consolidate or encounter a countercyclical correction. The following expands upon the behavior of primary bull and bear markets (uses weekly data).

- During primary bull markets, the average length of a period of consolidation is 13.8 months
- During primary bull markets, the average return for consolidation periods is 1.1 percent
- During primary bull markets, the median length of time for consolidation periods is 9 months
- During primary bull markets, the median return for consolidation periods is 0 percent
- During primary bull markets, the average countertrend return is -15 percent

- During primary bull markets, the median countertrend return is -13 percent
- During primary bull markets, the average length of time for a countertrend move is 7.25 months
- During primary bull markets, the median length of time for a countertrend move is 6 months.
- During primary bear markets, the average length of time for a consolidation period is 14.2 months
- During primary bear markets, the average return of a consolidation period is -1.1 percent
- During primary bear markets, the median length of time for a consolidation period is 11.5 months
- During primary bear markets, the median return of a period of consolidation is 0 percent
- During primary bear markets, the average countertrend return is 13.6 percent
- During primary bear markets, the median countertrend return is 13.4 percent
- During primary bear markets, the average length of time for a countertrend move is 6.7 months
- During primary bear markets, the median length of time for a countertrend is 5.5 months

There are several key takeaways from this data:

- Any sustained primary bull or primary bear market is interrupted with a countertrend move or a period of consolidation. Be ready for it so you don't react out of emotion.
- Countertrend moves in either primary bull or primary bear markets have a tendency to be uniform in percentage retracements as evidenced by the close average and median percentages.

- It is difficult to predict when a sideways consolidation move is going to end. For primary bull markets, the average duration length of a consolidation period is 13.8 months while the median is 9 months. For primary bear markets, the average duration length of a consolidation period is 14.2 months while the median is 11.5 months.

The countertrend move of the primary bull market that *began* in March of 2009 started in April of 2011 and continued through September of that year. Using weekly data, the decline from the top in April to the bottom in September was 15.6 percent. The average countertrend decline in a primary bull market is 15 percent. This correction lasted six months. The average duration is seven months and the median is six months. I remember giving a presentation to a group at the end of September suggesting that the market may have just ended an intermediate correction. The next month, the DJIA was up over 13 percent.

As part of my research, I also studied the movement of several financial variables during each primary, intermediate, and consolidation period. These financial variables include long-term interest rates, short-term interest rates, the consumer price index, changes in debt-to-GDP, and the movement of the US dollar. I will not go into depth regarding this portion of my research, but suffice it to say that key economic variables, such as the ones discussed above, behave differently in each primary market move. For example, the primary bull market from 1949 to 1961 that started after Truman entered the war against North Korea was characterized by a significant rise in short- and long-term interest rates, while the primary bull market between 1982 and 1999 was characterized by a significant decline in long- and short-term interest rates. But inflation, as measured by the consumer price index, was significantly higher between 1982 and 1999 than it was during the 1949 to 1961 time frame. Some primary bull markets are characterized by falling short-term and long-term rates, some are characterized by rising long-term and short-term rates, and others are characterized by declining long-term rates and rising short-term rates (such as the case with the primary bull market that started in April 1942 and ended in May 1946).

The benefit of understanding the tendencies of the various financial variables helps to dispel widely held beliefs that rising interest rates are bad for stocks and declining interest rates are eventually good for stocks. It is also widespread belief that the dollar gains when rates rise and dollar falls when rates drop. Interest rates were rising from 2003 to 2007, but the dollar fell anyway. In 1994 interest rates rose, but the dollar fell. In 1997 and 1998, rates dropped but the dollar rose. The answer, as always, depends on the environment.

A significant benefit of doing research of the market's historical tendencies of primary market moves and understanding how those primary moves unfold in terms of consolidation periods and countertrend moves is that it helps investors to better understand when an intermediate trend is happening based on a risk that is not likely to transpire and a primary longer-term trend that is based on a true change in fundamentals that lead to a temporary or more permanent change in economic equilibrium.

In primary moves, slow changes in fundamentals lead to changes in investor psychology; investor psychology always lags changes in the fundamentals. The reason why market prices "lead" the fundamentals is because *other* market participants who are superior at forecasting fundamental trends based on changes in the sociopolitical and economic conditions are the ones moving market prices. Prices have to move a great deal before individual investors as group grasp on to the fact that the economy is undergoing an equilibrium change.

In intermediate moves (within the primary trend), which seem a lot worse than they are, market action leads to changes in investor psychology, which leads to changes in the *perception* about the fundamentals. But when the perception about fundamentals proves unwarranted or the risk that that perception was based on does not transpire, the market quickly reverts back to the primary trend in force. I call these intermediate market corrections within primary uptrends "risk-based" corrections. Risk-based corrections have occurred all throughout history and therefore a norm. Some examples of these risk-based corrections include the Asian financial crisis in 1997, Russian financial crisis in 1998, collapse of Long Term Capital in 1998, Argentina's economic collapse in the early 2000s, Mexican financial collapse in 1995, Greek financial collapse in 2011, and the list goes on. During each of these examples, a stock market correction ensued but was relatively short-lived. It is these risk-based corrections that cause people to sell at the bottom. Fear is a very real emotion that is difficult to control and one that can be detrimental to your investment portfolio.

Other Notable Averages and Medians

Statistical averages can be used as a starting point, a basis from which to evaluate the risk of market involvement (Sperando 1991, 170). Below are some common averages and medians:

- The stock market leads the economy by an average of seven months at market tops.
- The stock market leads the economy by an average of five months at market bottoms.
- A bear market in stocks as defined by a 20 percent or greater correction occurs, on average every 5.2 years.
- Using post WWII data, the average decline and recovery (decline defined as 10 percent or more drop and the recovery defined as getting to the predecline level) cycle is 2.6 years. However, the range is .4 to 7.6 years
- The average P/E ratio for the S&P 500 for the past fifty years ending September 2009 is 16.4

How does one know if market prices are dropping due to a risk-based correction or a result of a true reordering of economic fundamentals? Or in a primary downtrend, how does one know if a short-lived increase in market prices is not going to result in a more sustained increase in the market? The best way to know the difference is to know when intermediate and primary trends are likely to occur and knowing the sociopolitical and economic events that can cause a change in equilibrium. This chapter's careful study of their occurrences, their time durations, and their magnitudes provides this valuable insight.

Chapter 14

MARKET AND INVESTOR PSYCHOLOGY

Understanding the psychology of the market in conjunction with a sense of where the market is in its progression within a primary bull or bear market will help self-aware investors overcome damaging emotional behaviors that lead to poor investment performance. Martin Pring (1991, 1) has summarized it the best:

> Success based on an emotional response to market conditions is the result of chance, and chance does not help us attain consistent results. Objectivity is not easy to achieve because all humans are subject to the vagaries of fear, greed, price of opinion, and all the other excitable states that prevent rational judgment. We can read books on various approaches to the market until our eyes are red and we can attend seminars given by experts, gurus, or anyone else who might promise us instant gratification, but all the market knowledge in the world will be useless without the ability to put this knowledge into action by mastering our emotions. We spend too much time trying to beat the market and too little time trying to overcome our frailties.

Part of overcoming detrimental emotions that cause irrational and detrimental investment decisions is learning to think for oneself and not taking at blind faith the opinion and dictations of others. Blind reliance upon "experts" and uncritical acceptance of popular catchwords and prejudices is tantamount to the abandonment of self-determination and to yielding to other people's domination (Mises 1963, 879).

I am a big fan of watching the A&E channel, particularly the show on hoarding where people have a sickness of collecting things. Maybe I like this show because I find this peculiar behavior so odd and am amazed by how many people cannot stop collecting junk. What does this have to do with investor psychology? Well, nothing really, except that the beginning of the show, the psycho therapist's first line of duty is to make the "patient" accept and own their sickness. The patient cannot be in denial that they have a hoarding problem if they are to get better. The same can be said about investors in general. To deny that you make emotional decisions is to accept mediocrity.

The objective of this chapter on market and investor psychology is twofold. First and foremost, is to bring *awareness* to investors that their prewired investment decision-making process can be detrimental to their own investment success. Secondly, once awareness exists investors need to *overcome* any denial that they may have with regard to having any consistent behavioral tendency toward making bad investment decisions.

You can't beat the market if you don't understand investor psychology

The market is efficient, but at the same time, it is not efficient. How can this be? Have you ever wondered why the market seems to do things that does not make sense, like go up after a string of negative earnings announcements or why the market goes down when most of the reported news is positive? Have you ever wondered why "overvalued" markets stay overvalued for periods of months, and sometimes years?

Have you ever wondered why "undervalued" markets stay undervalued for periods of months, and sometimes years? These questions would not arise if the market were always efficient.

The market is a discounting mechanism where historical and current, public and nonpublic information is factored into stock prices. If you agree with this argument, then you have no chance of "beating" the market. After all, if information, new and old, is already factored into stocks, it is impossible to beat the market unless you have access to information before anybody else is able to act on it.

To rectify this apparent contradiction, I believe that, on average, the market is efficient. If you take the extreme value at both ends, and divide their sum by two, I believe this is the appropriate valuation for the market at any given time. *But because we have extreme values to begin with implies that at certain times the market is not efficient.* Thus, there is an opportunity to beat the market if we are able to identify these extreme values and act on them. *Mass psychology causes these extreme values.*

Identifying extreme values (values that are significantly far from their mean) is an easy thing to do, but acting on them is very hard; greed and fear are strong manifestations of upside and downside extremes respectively. When metrics such as valuations, risk premiums, unemployment, or commodity prices reach upside and downside extremes, there will always be reasons why these values are justified at these levels. To complicate matters, there will always be examples of times when these extremes became bigger extremes and when they were sustained for a long periods of time. Deflation in Japan lasted almost twenty years. P/E ratios were double and triple their mean from 1999 to 2000. The subprime financial meltdown of 200[7]8 brought values down 50–75 percent in many financial stocks, far greater than what was thought to be possible. Acting and profiting from extreme values is not the easiest thing to do.

Given the unscientific nature of the stock market, and given that there will always be risks to any given viewpoint, people will always question a position they have taken. This is especially true when prices move against you. To compound this questioning, media reports will always paint a favorable view of the direction the market is taking. In other words, if prices are moving higher, the media will give ample explanations as to why. If prices are moving lower, the media will find plenty of reasons why that direction is justified. Thus, the media will cause you to question yourself even further.

The fact that many trends are operating simultaneously makes it very difficult to know if a short-term trend is an indication or the start of longer-term trend. For example, if you are betting on a price decline and the market moves higher, you would then begin to question whether you are on the wrong side of the market. Now, the market begins to move down in favor of your desired direction (but only after it moved against you 25 percent). Given that you probably already lost a lot of sleep after being down 25 percent, you begin to wonder if this small move in your desired direction is just a short-term blip. This will tempt you to sell and cut your losses once you have reached the breakeven point. Every trend is interrupted with corrections, but the start of a new trend always starts as a correction.

To take advantage of the inefficiencies of the market in an attempt to beat it requires understanding how the market works and the involvement that human emotion plays in that process. To complicate matters, the people who are able to beat the market do so at the expense of retail investors, who as a group are usually the ones that are wrong. I'm not saying these retail investors will lose money; they just won't beat the market. The people who consistently beat the market use the media and the media's effect on investor's psyche to their advantage and to the retail investor's detriment.

Market beaters also know how to take advantage of common knowledge of the marketplace. Just when investors think they have figured it out, "it" changes. There are traps built in to any kind of knowledge learned from observation.

To beat the market, you have to understand the weaknesses of market participants and be ready to act during times it is the most difficult. This may include buying after prices have gone up a lot (have you ever said to yourself, prices are too high?), cutting your losses after prices have gone down a lot (have you ever said I can't sell now, prices are too low?). This may also include buying when everybody else is selling and selling when everybody else is buying. You have to know when to join a trend and when to buck a trend. You have to know when to participate in the "common knowledge" of the marketplace and when to try and "outsmart" the market. Also, having knowledge of where the stock market is in its longer-term primary progression is very important as it will help you be patient and stay the course. *Patience is a virtue!*

Identify how to overcome all these weaknesses and you may be one step ahead in trying to beat the market. Hopefully this book will provide you with some valuable tools and methodologies that will allow you to sell when others are buying, buy when others are selling, join an already established trend (assuming the trend will continue), and stay the course during times that make these actions most advantageous to do so.

The biggest form of detrimental behavior that individual investors as group exhibit is having beliefs that are so strong that it clouds their ability to make sound and objective investment decisions. As such, it will be worthwhile to explore where some of these beliefs come from.

Beliefs

Most investors have their own beliefs that have been shaped through years of political affiliation, formal education, cultural experiences, business experiences, etc. It is through this lens that a personal understanding of the world is shaped. However, an understanding of what ought to be is different than an understanding of what is. This is the classical difference between normative and positive economics. Positive economics is in principle independent of any ethical or normative judgments as it deals with what is, not what ought to be. Laymen and experts alike are inevitably tempted to shape positive conclusions to fit strongly held normative preconceptions and to reject positive conclusions if their normative implications—or what are said to be their normative implications—are unpalatable (Friedman 1953, 4). Because differences in viewpoints exist and since they can potentially be damaging due to gaps between these viewpoints and their effect on asset prices, it is worthwhile to explore where some of these viewpoints originate with the hope that investors can see through their weaknesses.

Glass Half Full versus Glass Half Empty

Probably the most important source of bias has to do with one's own emotional makeup. In my years of working with retail clients and having sat through thousands of meetings, I have noticed a sharp distinction between people who are predisposed to skepticism and those who are predisposed to optimism. However, this is not to say that skeptics are never optimistic and that optimists are never skeptical. Rather, I am referring to a general state of reference that must be proven wrong before an alternative view will be accepted.

All the knowledge in the world cannot make up for not having the emotional fortitude to engage in the necessary behaviors to achieve investment success. Understanding one's own predisposition toward optimism and skepticism and taking steps to counter these biases is necessary if one is to have any consistency in their own investment returns. Any investor striving to make better investment decisions has to achieve emotional balance. According to Tony Schwartz (Schwartz 2010, 30), "Honesty in the absence of compassion becomes cruelty. Tenacity unmediated by flexibility congeals into rigidity. Confidence untempered by humility is arrogance. Courage without prudence is recklessness. Because all virtues are connected to others, any strength overused ultimately becomes a liability." It is healthy to ask what can go wrong when the market takes on an invincible persona. Conversely, it is healthy to ask what can go right during times of economic and financial collapse. A little self-awareness can go a long way!

But Beliefs Are Okay

It is perfectly normal to have a bias toward a certain philosophical approach if one has a self-awareness that this bias in belief exists. However, danger occurs when these beliefs become so ingrained that it becomes emotional; it becomes even more dangerous when one is not aware of this emotion. In addition, biased assumptions become very dangerous if one rationalizes acceptance of this assumption in light of counter evidence, a problem that is notorious among professional economists. These normative assumptions influence the choice of subjects that economists study and the answers they will accept (Gilpin 2001, 65). For example, a mortgage underwriter who use to sit in the office next to mine was losing money hand over fist because of his glass-half-empty bias. During the second quarter of 2009, he was short the commercial real estate market all the while ignoring all the technical signs including the fact that a new uptrend had just been confirmed. He failed to see that the market had been discounting another Great Depression that did not occur and that commercial real estate was never as over built as residential real estate. Moreover, he under appreciated the fact that developers and bankers were more willing to negotiate rent payments to avoid what had happened to residential real estate. In sum, he did not have an awareness of his own grim view of the world.

When Beliefs Can Become Truth

In addition to understanding one's own biased beliefs and countering these biases with a healthy dose of self-awareness, it is important to realize that not everybody has an awareness of how little truth there can be in their own preconceived views of how the world should work. *Most people think that their philosophies and views work in every single sociopolitical context; it takes a real thinker to admit that in some contexts their philosophies just don't work.* I am appalled by how many people I have come into contact with throughout the financial crisis of 2008 and its aftermath who proclaimed that higher taxes will be the death nail for the market. The historical record certainly does not suggest that. Marginal income tax rate increases occurred in 1918, 1932, 1952, 1990, and 1993. In all of these situations, the stock market was up during the entire time period consisting of the rest of that year (the year of the tax hike) and all of the next. But because so many people have opinions and philosophies, that may or may not work in that given context, these opinions and philosophies must be understood because they affect behavior and behavior affects consumer and investing decisions. For Keynes, "rational interest" and economic interests are not based upon "given" interests but on intuitive beliefs. Consequently, interests are "fickle" things that behave nonrationally and are constituted by ideas (Blyth 2002, 42). Mark Blyth (2002, vii–viii) succinctly summarizes this point:

> Bought into a series of ideas that not only shaped his interests, but did so irrespective of their truth content. This led me to the idea that so long as something about the economy is believed by a large enough group of people, then because they believe it, it becomes true. So if being

believed is functionally equivalent to being true, then belief itself becomes politically and economically efficacious. Ideas therefore do not "really" need to correspond to the "real" world in order to be important in that world.

We should all be self-aware of our self-awareness and aware of the lack of self- awareness of others and how that lack of self- awareness, if widespread, can affect consumer and investment decisions.

In the following section, I will identify some of the more common biases that cause investors to underperform. The best way to combat these destructive emotional tendencies is to be aware of them.

What Biases Cause Retail Investors as a Group to Systematically Underperform?

Too Much Belief in the Media

Individual investors are fooled into thinking that media accounts of the causes of market action are truly the causes. When do the media ever report good news when the market goes down? Similarly, when do the media report bad news when the market goes up? There are sure to be positive economic developments when the market is going down, but we will never hear of them. *The market has a law of its very own and the media's involvement in that law oftentimes seems like a plot against the retail investor to take advantage of the frailties of fear and greed.* In fundamentally difficult environments, people are more careful about how they spend and invest their money because money is much more difficult to come by. According to Bill Bonner (2006, 2 – 3):

> Watching the news is a bit like watching a bad opera. You can tell from all the shrieking that something very important is supposed to be happening, but you don't

quite know what it is. What you are missing is the plot... the characters on stage are familiar to us—consumers, economists, politicians, investors, and businessmen. They are the same hustlers, clowns, rubes, and dumbbells that we always see before us...but, people come to believe whatever they must believe when they must believe it..... As they say on Wall Street, "markets make opinions," not the other way around.

Fear and Greed

Individual investors have a tendency to be overly greedy near the top of a market and overly fearful near the bottom. During a sharp parabolic rise in an asset's price, it is very easy for investors to be envious of those who got in early and have made a lot of money by participating in the rise. Suddenly, all sound reason is thrown out of the window, and one chooses to forget about the disconnection between the asset's price and underlying fundamentals and instead just wants to make money while the price is rising. During this phase of greed, people begin believing the so-called experts who are spouting reasons why the asset should be that high and why the price should even go higher. A market prognosticator in 2004 predicted the DJIA to be at forty thousand and the NASDAQ to be at twenty thousand. In 2006, I had a conversation with a family member who justified the doubling and tripling of real estate in Arizona as finally catching up to California real estate prices, where it should have been a long time ago. I remember thinking to myself if that were the case, then Arizona real estate prices would have been at the same level as real estate in California a long time ago. I also remember thinking to myself that California has nice beaches while Arizona does not.

Fear is an equally powerful emotion. When prices are dropping relentlessly, there is no shortage of opinion as to why prices can't drop further. At this phase, investors begin thinking about what would happen if they had to adjust their lifestyle to match their now smaller financial portfolio and the lifestyle that they would have to live if their portfolio dropped even more. At one point during 2008, I had a client ask me what would happen if the stock market dropped to zero!

Changes When You Least Expect It

Individual investors are also notorious for thinking that past habits of the market will repeat the same way each time presented with a similar situation. In the language of behavioral finance, academics have coined this phenomenon recency bias. Market habits will change when you least expect it. I routinely track investor sentiment to see the rate of change of the level of bullishness or bearishness in the market. From 2009 to the end of 2011, almost every instance where the level of bullishness had an abnormal increase, the market sold off during the weeks that followed. Similarly, when the level of bearishness had an abnormal increase, the market would rise in the following weeks. An already bruised and battered individual investor was getting whipsawed. I suspect that once the market senses that the retail investor has caught on to this play on their emotions, they will throw in the towel and give up; this will be when the market will achieve its greatest gains.

I'm All In, No, Wait I'm All Out

Most individual investors don't understand that reduced volatility can help achieve superior investment returns. Moving all in or all out of the market each time you have an opinion on its direction is a recipe for volatility. Let's assume investor A has a $1MM and makes a 100 percent return the first year but gets completely out of the market the next year and earns 0 percent in that second year. The portfolio value at the end of year two is $2MM and the average return is 50 percent. Investor B has a $1MM and makes a 50 percent return the first year and a 50 percent return the second year. The average is still 50 percent, but investor B has $2.25MM. A balanced investment strategy with a narrower band of investment return possibilities is always better than an all-in or all-out strategy.

My CPA Told Me Not To Do It

Individual investors like to let taxes dictate what they do. Just like a dog's tail does not wag the dog, taxes should not be the sole reason to keep a position. More often than not, hanging on to a position with embedded gains, especially if that position represents a concentrated position, does not represent an ideal risk and return. Having worked with many corporate executives during 1999 and 2000, I saw many concentrations result in millions of dollars from stock options and restricted stock being compounded exponentially for years. This outcome is not likely to come to fruition over the next decade or two. I remember meeting with a young Intel executive after the Tech Wreck of 2000 who asked me how he can make millions like his boss and his boss's boss? I told him he had to do it the old-fashioned way.

Loss Aversion

Individual investors exhibit a great deal of loss aversion. Loss aversion is the tendency for investors to avoid losses than to acquire gains (Pompian 2006, 208). Loss aversion is a bias that simply cannot be tolerated in financial decision making. It instigates the exact opposite of what investors want: increased risk with lower returns. Investors should take risk to increase gains, not to mitigate losses. Holding losers and selling winners will wreak havoc on a portfolio (211).

When Philosophy and Behavior Diverge

Individual investors in many cases don't properly align their behavior with their investment philosophy. For example, saying you are a trader but not taking the time to analyze and monitor your positions and then blaming your lack of time for poor investment results. Similarly, saying that you are a long-term investor but having a trader mentality and wanting to move in and out of the market on a daily and weekly basis. Or to claim that you are a day trader but rationalize holding on to positions because you don't like to sell for a loss. There is more than one successful way to invest, but some methods have more chance for success than others. But choosing a method and acting in a different manner will always lead to failure.

Rationalizing the Irrational

Individual investors like to rationalize the irrational. Knowing something isn't right but trying to frame a situation to fit an emotional feeling is what I call rationalizing the irrational. I had a client in October 2008 direct me to sell all his equities because he did not like the direction the country was going. Before he was my client, he had lost over two-thirds of his portfolio in the Tech Wreck and was emotionally scarred by that sudden and drastic reduction in his wealth. As a result, he rationalized what he knew was the wrong course of action. On the flipside, I had another client who was almost all cash, and every time I would present nice well-researched reasons for investing, he would say, "Let's wait and see what the market does."

Overconfidence

Individual investors also have a tendency to display a great deal of overconfidence in their investment decision making. Of course most people who have the wealth to participate in the stock market have achieved their wealth through business and educational success. A commonality among these investors is the sense that business and educational success should endow them with superior investment decision making when it comes to stocks. But running a business, a corporate division, or getting through the long and tenuous process of medical school couldn't be more different than making alpha-generating investment decisions. In short, overconfidence bias is when people think they are smarter and have better information than they actually do… one general implication of overconfidence bias in any form is that overconfident investors may not be well prepared for the future (Pompian 2006, 51–61).

There are many more systemic fragilities associated with human investment decision making that are too numerous to discuss in this book. These fragilities will be the main reasons why retail investors as a group will be eaten alive by more savvy hedge funds, day traders, and proprietary traders if left unchecked. When you have finally gotten fed up with the volatility of the market and the market dropping when you feel good about the economy or the market rising when you see no ray of hope, the market may experience a sustained period of positive returns. Once you have missed out on this sustained period of positive returns and finally commit money to the market, the market may finally decide to stop going up. My purpose in this chapter is not to dissuade investors from investing in the market. In fact, my motivation is the opposite, this is a good time to invest money, but the old rules have changed and a multifaceted approach is necessary to succeed. Understand the landscape, understand the players in the market, understand your own weaknesses, have a multivaried approach to decision making, and you can win in this fundamentally difficult environment.

Elliott Wave

So far I have covered the necessity of understanding the role of investor psychology in beating the market. In sum, investor psychology is so emotionally ingrained that it clouds judgment. All of these human emotional and cognitive tendencies have repetitive form. R.N. Elliott recognized these repetitions early on and has researched these forms. Robert Prechter Jr. advanced the early work of R.N. Elliott into what is known today as Elliott Wave. According to Prechter (2005, 21):

> Sometimes the market appears to reflect outside conditions and events, but at other times it is entirely detached from what most people assume are causal conditions. The reason is that the market has a law of its own. It is not propelled by the external causality to which one becomes accustomed in everyday life. The path of prices is not a product of news. Nor is the market the cyclicality rhythmic machine that some declare it to be. Its movement reflects a repetition of forms that is independent both of presumed causal events and of periodicity.

As part of his research, Prechter does a great job summarizing the social mood and emotional feeling at various points within primary bull and bear stock market cycles. For a complete review of his seminal work on the behavior the market, you should read *Elliott Wave Principle: Key to Market Behavior* or *R.N. Elliott's Master Works: The Definitive Collection*.

Market Top

There are various degrees of declines in the stock market. What is valuable to know is the emotional or psychological state of mind that accompanies small drops, intermediate-sized drops, and large drops in the stock market. According to Prechter, large drops in the stock market are typically associated with a general feeling that prosperity and peace will be guaranteed forever and arrogant complacency reigns. Intermediate drops in the market are usually associated with economic improvement and good feeling. Minor drops often accompanied by good news (Prechter and Frost, 2006, pp82).

Market Bottom

There are also various degrees of stock market rises. At key market bottoms that usually accompany strong and sustained stock market recoveries, Prechter and Frost note that the general feeling is a question of survival, depression, and war. At intermediate rises in the stock market, the general feeling is recession, panic, and limited wars. And minor rallies are often accompanied by bad news (Prechter and Frost, 2006, pp 83).

The biggest fortunes are made by doing two things: getting out near the top before the start of a primary bear market and getting in near the bottom before the start of a primary bull market. Unfortunately, these fortunes aren't made by retail investors. They are made by people who embody the mind-set of men like Warren Buffet and George Soros. Having emotions of fear, greed, beliefs, optimism, pessimism, and overconfidence all at the wrong time prevent most of us from doing what we know we must do—buy low and sell high. However, being aware of your own weaknesses and emotions and overcoming them can put you on the right path to changing the way you think so you can make better investment decisions.

Chapter 15

CYCLES

Cycles are another important component of market behavior. Cycles can help us determine if something truly fundamental is occurring in the market or if it is just an aberration. After analyzing the market's historical tendencies, market psychology, technical analysis, and a fundamental analysis, and one is still unsure of the market's primary direction, a cycle analysis may be the determining factor in forecasting the market's trend. I approach the market's cyclical tendencies with the assumption that they will occur as scheduled unless there is any good fundamental reason why they shouldn't. One must be careful, however, in making investment decisions based solely on a cyclical tendency because the tendency may not occur. I much prefer using a cyclical analysis in conjunction with other analytical tools to obtain a sense of the *primary* market trend. According to Jeffrey and Yale Hirsch (2012, 4), when referring to their Stock Trader's Almanac, "The Almanac is a practical investment tool. It alerts you to those little-known market patterns and tendencies on which shrewd professionals enhance profit potential." For more information on stock market cycles, I recommend picking up the *Stock Trader's Almanac*.

Seasonality

Common cycles have to do with seasonality where certain days, months, and seasons of the year have a tendency to outperform or underperform other months and seasons. For example, the winter quarter consisting of November, December, and January is the best three-month period of the year. August and September are typically the two worst months of the year. During August of 2011, the DJIA started what would eventually become a 15 percent decline due to problems occurring in Greece. The sovereign bonds of Greece were trading at 50 percent of par value because of liquidity concerns arising from their inability to receive reasonable financing for debt that was maturing. There was fear of a sovereign default and how that would spread through the rest of Europe, particularly the large number of banks that held Greek debt. However, the issues pertaining to Greece was nothing new. In fact, the market knew more than a year prior to August 2011 that a liquidity crunch and potential default would be inevitable. Headlines from the *New York Times* from May through August of 2010 reported "Fumbling Toward Default: Europe's approach to the Greek debt crisis remains far too blinkered and passive," "Standard and Poor's warns bank plan will cause Greek default," "High and Low Finance: Inevitability of a default in Greece." At this point, the astute investor does not know if the market correction that became more acute in August 2011 was something truly related to the possibility of a default in Greece or if it were just a cyclical tendency that would eventually fix itself.

Going back to our earlier discussion about historical tendencies of the market, we knew that, using month-end data for the DJIA that the average return for a primary bull market was 208 percent and the average duration was fifty-eight months. The high point using month-end data for the DJIA in 2011 was 12,830. The return from the March 9, 2009, bottom (again using month-end data) of 7,095 is a gain of 81 percent. The duration of the primary bull market that started in March of 2009 through April 2011 was twenty-five months. The returns and the duration of the primary bull market that led up to the correction in August were far less than the average. This was suggestive that the decline was a temporary cyclical blip instead of the start of another long and devastating market drop. Moreover, using Robert Prechter's framework of market psychology there was a sense of "economic improvement and good feeling," which aptly described the emotion in April 2011 when the market topped out for the year. Some headlines in the *New York Times* from March 2011 through April 2011 include "Fed Report Says Economy Continues Moderate Growth," "U.S. Posts Gains in Jobs of 216,000 a Boost for President Obama," "Economic Growth More Robust than Earlier Estimated." As it turned out, the market staged an intermediate bottom in late September to stage one of the best Octobers that history has ever seen.

The best known book for seasonal and annual cyclical tendencies is Jeffrey and Yale Hirsch's Stock Trader's Almanac, which is published every year.

- The first five days of January in election years; a record of 13–2 (Hirsch 2012, 14). In election years if the first five trading days have positive returns so will the rest of the year. If the first five days is negative so will be the rest of the year.
- January barometer states that as the S&P 500 goes in January, so goes the rest of the year. The last thirty-eight up first five days were followed by full year gains thirty-three times, for an 86.8 percent accuracy ratio and a 13.9 percent average gain in all thirty-eight years (Hirsch 2012, 14).
- The best three-month period for the market is November, December, and January.

- The top performing individual months for the DJIA are April, November, and December (Hirsch 2012, 44).
- The best six months of the year between November 1 and April 30
- Since 1987, August is the worst month for the DJIA (Hirsch 2012, 72).
- Expanding the time frame to include years before 1987, September is the worst month and April is the best month (Hirsch 2012, 44).
- Since 1952, all but two instances the DJIA fell on average 10.9 percent when the December low was breached in the first quarter of the following year. Only three significant drops occurred when December's low was not breached in Q1 (1974, 1981, and 1987) (Hirsch 2012, 40).

Four-Year Presidential Cycle

The four-year presidential cycle consists of a pattern of stock market returns that has recurred frequently throughout history. The return pattern from best to worst occurs as follows: pre-election year, election year, midterm year, postelection year. The fact that there are certain presidential cycle tendencies to begin with strikes right to the heart of the importance of politics and its emotional effect on society as a whole. It is no mere coincidence that election years and pre-election years (2012 and 2011) of the forty-four administrations since 1833 produced a total net market gain of 718.5 percent, dwarfing the 273 percent gain of the first two years (postelection and midterm years) of these administrations (Hirsch 2012, 130). When referring to election years, Hirsch (2012, 24) notes the following:

- Regardless of which party is victorious in election years, the last seven months have seen gains on the S&P in thirteen of the fifteen presidential elections since 1950. Exceptions were in 2000 and 2008.

- First five months better when party retains White House. Since 1901 there have been twenty-seven presidential elections. During the sixteen times the party in power retained the White House, the Dow was up 1.5 percent on average for the first five months, compared to a 4.6 percent loss the eleven times the party was ousted.

- A takeover of the White House by the opposing party in the past fifty years (1960, 1968, 1976, 1980, 1992, 2000, 2008) has resulted in a bottom within two years, except 1994, a flat year. When the incumbent parties retained power (1964, 1972, 1984, 1988, 1996, 2004) stocks often bottom within two years as well except 1984 (three years, 1987) and 2004 (one year flat, 2005). Whatever the outcome in 2012, we could see a bottom in 2014.

- There have only been six election year declines greater than 5 percent since 1896.

- Markets tend to be stronger when party in power wins

The Kondratieff Wave

The Kondratieff Wave is a long-term cycle that was originally discovered by Russian economist, Nikolai Kondratieff. Essentially this long-term cycle last approximately sixty years and is broken up into four components each lasting about fifteen years. Each component of this sixty-year cycle is named after the four seasons—spring, summer, autumn, and winter. Kondratieff documented that economic cycles of modern capitalist countries tend to repeat a cycle of expansion and contraction lasting a bit over half a century (Prechter 2005, 185).

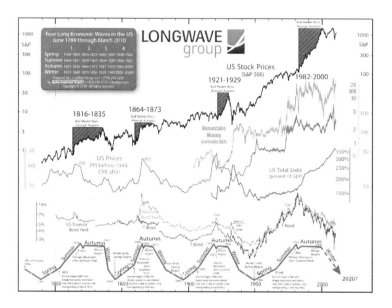

Source: Long Wave Group

In describing the recent sixty year cycle, John Murphy (2004, 197) explains:

> The notations in the above Kondratieff Wave are the work of Ian Gordon. The spring season from 1949 to 1966 is characterized by a strengthening economy and benign inflation when stocks do well. Summer begins in 1966 and ends in 1980 is an inflationary period and is marked by rising commodity prices, gold, and real estate. Autumn, beginning in 1980 sees the greatest speculation in bonds, stocks, and real estate. This speculative era also seems a massive buildup of debt. Gordon puts the start of the Kondratieff winter in 2000. The main characteristic of the economic winter (marked by a collapse in commodity prices) is deflation, which is made worse by the need to repay all of the debt built up during the autumn period. Stock prices plunge (as do real estate prices)… Because of its length is approximately 60 years, Gordon describes

the Kondratieff Wave as a *lifetime cycle* because most people live through it only once. This explains why each generation is unprepared for its onset—and unfamiliar with its solutions.

The copyright date of the above caption is 2004 and what a prediction it was. Whether you put the start of the winter season of the most recent cycle in 2000 or 2007, there is one thing that is clear: it is going to be a very long winter! Typically, the winter will be characterized by a devastated sociopolitical and economic environment. It will take a long time for confidence to be restored. It will take a new generation of business leaders and spenders, who did not experience the prior winter's tumult, to rise on the scene and take risk. Then the spring starts the cycle all over again.

Other Notable Cyclic Tendencies of the Market

- The ten-year treasury yield has a tendency to go up during the first six months of the year and down the last six months of the year. So when the media marches on about why rates are rising, just know that this cyclic tendency exists.
- The business cycle has a tendency to produce a recession every four years; however, it is not always on time. Recessions: 1970, 1974, 1980, 1982, 1990, and 2001. Sometimes a stock market may produce a bear market in anticipation of a recession, but no such recession may occur. For example, 1994. Furthermore, the economy missed its scheduled recession in 1986, but the market dropped in 1987.
- The US dollar has a tendency to reach important bottoms in January.

Question and Answer

Question: (End January 2012) I have some cash that I
  want to invest, how would you suggest I go about it?
Answer: January has been a very good month. In
  election years, the majority of the market returns
  are concentrated in the last seven months of the
  year. I see no reason why this will not be the case
  this year. Since each of the next four months are
  not going to duplicate January's great returns, I
  suspect that there is going to be some volatility and
  a correction going into the second half of the year. I
  would take that volatility as a chance to get some of
  that cash invested according to your desired target
  asset allocation.

Chapter 16

TECHNICAL ANALYSIS

Technical analysis is the study of historical price patterns that have predictive value in forecasting the future direction of market prices. I would extend this definition to include other derivations from price data such as momentum and volume. As they say, *a picture is worth a thousand words*. Whether you believe in the value of technical analysis or not, one thing is sure: because there is a very large following of its predictive capabilities, technical analysis has branched off to form its own discipline. Steve Nison (2001, 11) has summarized:

> The importance of technical analysis is multifaceted. First, while fundamental analysis may provide a gauge of the supply / demand situations (i.e. price / earnings ratios, economic statistics), and so forth, there is no psychological component involved in such analysis. Yet, the markets are influenced at times, to a major extent, by emotionalism. As John Maynard Keynes stated, "there is nothing so disastrous as a rational investment policy in an irrational world." Technical analysis provides the only mechanism to measure the "irrational" (emotional) component present in all markets.

This chapter focuses on some of the basic concepts of technical analysis that I have found most useful in determining the end and beginning of primary market moves. Although technical analysis is very expansive, I will focus only on the tools most useful for broad market forecasting. Although I use technical analysis to obtain a broad understanding of the market's overall direction, these same concepts can be applied toward individual stock analysis as well.

Before we go further, I want to refute a common use of technical analysis. Many believe that technical analysis is strictly for the day trader who is in and out of the stock market hourly and daily. Although many technical analysis concepts are designed for high frequency trading, there are many other more practical application of technical analysis for purposes of broad market forecasting.

Data Frequency

Monthly data charts are used for longer-term forecasting, such as forecasting that extends out a year or more. Intermediate charts that use weekly data points are for forecasting time periods between three to twelve months. Daily charts are typically used for short-term forecasting. Given that our whole purpose is broad market forecasting, we will pay most of our attention in this chapter to monthly and weekly charts.

Chart 16.1 Monthly chart of the DJIA for the period January 2008 to January 2012

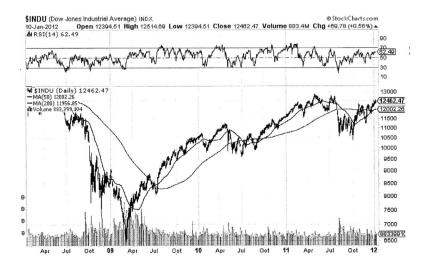

16.3 Daily chart of the DJIA between January 2008 to January 2012

As you can see in the above charts that cover the time frame January 2008 to January 2012, the longer-term charts smooth out the gyrations that one typically sees in the shorter-term charts. Daily charts typically use the end of the day price as the data point. Weekly charts typically use Friday's close as the data point. Monthly charts typically use the end of the month's (assuming the end of the month does not fall on a holiday or weekend) data point. Part of longer-term broad market forecasting is to sort out the noise that is inherent in short-term stock price movement. As such, using only monthly or weekly data points is better because the charts appear much "smoother." In sum, use monthly data frequency charts first to obtain a "longer-term" sense of the market and use weekly data frequency charts to obtain an "intermediate-term" sense of the market.

Data Display

Since the market has continuous and perpetual pricing, at what point in time is the price captured on the chart? Is it the opening price, the closing price, the average price, or any other random price for the time period in question? These are all valid questions, and I will cover briefly the two main data display options that are most useful.

Straight Line

Straight line charts are pretty self-explanatory as they represent one data entry per period—daily, weekly, or monthly. These data points are then charted on a graph. Following is an example of a straight line chart.

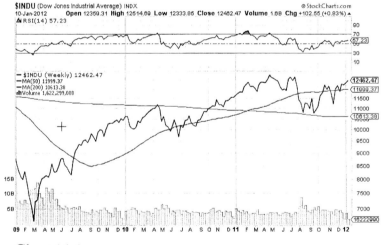

Chart 16.4

Japanese Candlesticks

Japanese candlestick charts are my preference for data display. Japanese candlestick charts represent the open, high, low, and close data for the month, week, or day; and it does so in a way that allows one to easily visualize the "emotion" and "character" of the market. These visualizations are powerful.

Below is an example of weekly candlestick chart covering the period January 2011–January 2012:

Chart 16.5

The rectangular portion of each week is called the *real body*. The real body represents the range between the open and the close. A candle that is "filled in" means the close was lower than the open. A candle that is white (empty) means the close for the week was higher than the open. A very long candle represents a great deal of either pessimism (when filled in) or optimism (when empty). The lines above and below the rectangles represent the extreme values for the period in question (in this case the period is a week). These lines are called shadows. Very small real bodies, but long shadows represent a great deal of indecision on behalf of market participants as there was significant movement only to have the market close near the open. The combination of real bodies and shadows for daily charts represent the daily action while monthly candle charts represent the monthly action.

Comparing the straight line chart with the Japanese candlestick chart, one can easily see why I prefer the latter. The Japanese candlestick charts paint a more compelling story.

Resistance

Resistance represents a price level or area *over* the market where selling pressure overcomes buying pressure and a price advance is turned back (Murphy 1999, 55). Resistance points are important because, in a primary *bear* market, these points can provide a sense of when countertrend prices increases will stop. In primary *bull* markets, resistance points are important because they provide a sense of when a new primary trend in the opposite direction may start. There are a many ways to record resistance areas on a price chart for a particular market. I will review a few of the more common methods to determine resistance.

Previous Price Peaks

Chart 16.6

Previous price peaks serve as resistance and usually represent critical junctures in the market's primary advance. Using the above illustration, you can see that the DJIA made a high in May 2010 before it retreated. In November of that year, the DJIA once again advanced toward the 11,200 resistance area. This time, the DJIA failed to break above this level upon initial approach. In fact, the DJIA spent a few weeks hovering around 11,200. At this point, one would be concerned about whether another retreat from this level was imminent. However, Santa Clause appeared in good graces and drove the market above this resistance in December of that year. In April of 2011, the DJIA reached a weekly closing high at around 12,800; this level was tested in August and unfortunately the DJIA was not able to surpass it. Instead, a short-lived correction of moderate magnitude took the DJIA down just over 15 percent. In order for the market to continue its advance, it is paramount that this resistance area be broken. When sellers do not come in to drive prices lower at these resistance levels symbolizes that the fundamental environment is strong enough to drive the market higher. In sum, a sustained break above a previous high is a sign the previous uptrend will continue. A failed attempt at making a new high is usually taken as a warning sign.

Downtrend Line

Chart 16.7

A downtrend line connects the lower highs associated with a market in decline. In order for a downtrend to occur, a series of lower highs is necessary. A line connecting the tops of these lower highs is called a downtrend line. Illustration 16.7 is a great example of a downtrend line that was eventually broken. It is common for a trend line to be broken initially only to fall back below such as what occurred in June of 2001. I call this a false breakout. This downtrend line was tested on five different occasions and finally broke above it in a sustainable fashion in October 2003. An upside breakout from a downtrend line that has lasted a long time and has been tested several times is symbolic of a market that has significant upside potential.

Broken Support Becomes Resistance

The opposite of resistance is support. When the market drops, eventually there comes a level where buyers come in to prop up prices. Some support levels are stronger than others just as some resistance levels are stronger than others. During a market decline, when key support levels are broken, those levels become resistance. Think about this. When prices are dropping and buyers, who have historically come in to support market prices are nowhere to be found, it is an indication that something more fundamental in the environment is occurring. But given that support areas are known by many market participants, you have a significant amount of buying that occurs at these support levels with the idea that prices will hold at these levels and begin to rise. The market will then spend a few weeks hovering around and perhaps even rise slightly at this level of support, and all the sudden, like gravity gave way, the market sinks right through this support level. Everybody who bought at this level of support is now losing money.

Now the view changes. These same investors vow to get out at breakeven. This breakeven point is the same level of support that caused the purchase to begin with. Thus, this potential for mass selling at this level of breakeven now becomes resistance.

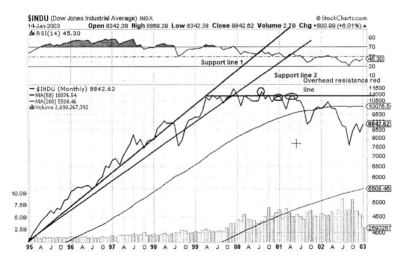

Chart 16.8

There are two support lines connecting a series of higher lows. Support line 1 connects three higher lows in the DJIA that occurred on July 1996, March 1997, and October 1997. This support line was broken June 1998. Broken support lines become resistance. Notice that in April of 1999 the DJIA approached the support line that was extended by connecting the three reactionary lows stated earlier. But the DJIA was not able to break above that line. Although the market continued higher, what started in 1999 was a series of higher lows that were of lower trajectory than the series used to connect support line 1. See support line 2. This should have been taken as the first sign of market weakness. You might wonder why I drew a line right through the market drop that occurred in August 1998. This is a false break down where the market quickly rallied above the broken support line and went on to make a series of higher lows. Support line 2 connects the series of higher lows that occurred after this false break down.

The strength of the resistance area seen in the horizontal line in chart 16.8 is due to two things. First is the break below support line 1(which now becomes resistance) and the subsequent test of this line (the DJIA approached this line but did not break above it). The second is the level in which support line 2 was broken. The test of support line 1 (April 1999 as mentioned earlier) and the break below of support line 2 occurred at roughly the same price level of 11,000 on the DJIA. The straight horizontal line in the above chart represents overhead resistance. The three small circles in chart 16.8 represent three successful tests of this resistance. A sustained break above any resistance level should be taken as a good sign. A failure to break above a resistance area, especially after a prolonged primary bull market, should be taken as a warning the uptrend may be coming to an end. The resistance that was formed in this example was the start of a three-year primary bear market in stocks.

Support

Support is the exact opposite of resistance. In the words of John Murphy (1999, 55):

> The troughs or reaction lows are called support. The term is self-explanatory and indicates that support is a level or area on the chart *under* the market where buying interest is sufficiently strong to overcome selling pressure. As a result, a decline is halted and prices turn back up again. Usually a support level is identified beforehand by a previous reaction low.

During a primary bull market support levels are important because you have a sense of what price levels countertrend declines will stop. During a primary bear market support levels are important because they provide a sense of when a decline in stocks will end.

Previous Price Troughs

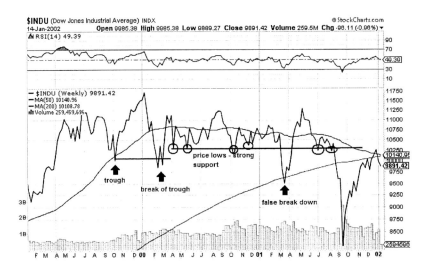

Chart 16.9

Using chart 16.9 for illustration and moving from left to right:

- Trough: first low
- Break of trough: the previous low was broken suggesting further downside. However, this was a false break down since the DJIA quickly advanced above the previous price low of 10,000.
- Price lows—strong support: starting in April of 2000 and extending into September of 2001, the DJIA established a very strong base of support at around 10,350. This support level was tested six times before it was decisively broken.
- False break down: In June of 2001, the DJIA broke below the previous four reactionary lows. This was a significant break as the DJIA dropped an additional 10 percent (as opposed to a small and short break, which are common) below the support level that connected the previous four lows. At this juncture, it would have been common for investors to reduce risk. Over the course of the next three months, however, the DJIA then rallied above this same support level. The level of volatility around this support level was a clear signal that something was not right. If the market were so healthy, why would it have dropped so much at this key area to begin with? Support and resistance levels have to be treated with caution; they don't always hold as false breakouts and breakdowns are common in financial markets. However, the concept of support and resistance, used in conjunction with other tools and methodologies gives one a better sense of how to interpret and react to these false break outs and breakdowns as they are occurring in real time.
- The final straw came in July of 2001 as the DJIA not only broke below the support line (reference chart 16.9), but it also breached the previous reactionary low formed in

June of that year. At this juncture, full defensive posturing would have been the wisest course of action.

Uptrend Line

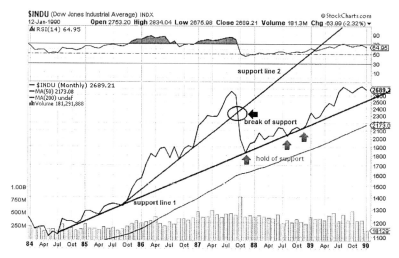

Chart 16.10

An uptrend line connects the higher lows associated with a rising market. In chart 16.10 you see support line 1, which is a longer-term support line formed by connecting the four higher lows—July 1984, November 1984, April 1985, and September 1985—and extending this line out. Support line 2 is an intermediate term support line formed during the DJIA's accelerated uptrend that lasted from the third quarter of 1985 to the fourth quarter of 1987. Support line 2 was formed by connecting the higher lows that occurred in September 1985, September 1986, and November 1986. A break below support line 2 occurred on Monday, October 19, 1987, on a day that has gone down in history as Black Monday when the market declined by more than 20 percent in one day. This illustration is a good example of using support to know when a market decline will stop; the DJIA stopped at the long-term support line (support line 1). This illustration is also a good example of using a broken support level to reduce risk such as the case when support line 2 was violated. The concept of support is helpful in primary bull markets because it provides one with a sense of how low countertrend declines will go. In addition, the concept of support is helpful in primary bear markets because it provides one with a sense of when a primary market decline may stop.

Previous resistance is now support

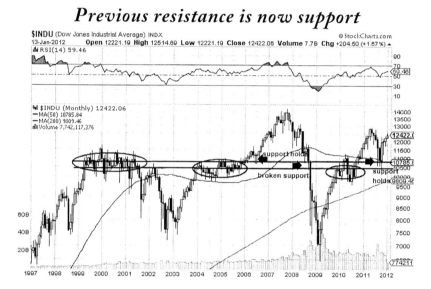

Chart 16.11

When the market breaks above a resistance level, that level then turns into support. Those investors who sold short at resistance lose money when the market rises above that level. As such, when the market drops again toward that same former resistance level, short covering occurs as investors seek to break even.

In chart 16.11 I have circled three resistance areas and drawn a line through the middle that represents the average price for each month (this chart is a monthly Japanese candlestick chart that represents the months high, low, open, and close). The first circle represents the price level in which the market spent two years hovering around. The second circle represents the price level in which the market spent two years hovering around. The third circle represents the price level in which the market spent one year hovering around. Collectively, the DJIA spent five years hovering around the area between 10,450 and 10,850. This zone represents an important area of support. Notice how each break above or below this zone results in a significant move.

Broken resistance turns into support. During 2003, the DJIA industrial average encountered a significant challenge breaking above the prior resistance area noted above. The DJIA spent nearly all of 2004 and 2005 hovering around 10,450 to 10,850 before the final push above, which occurred in January 2006. The level between 10,850 and 10,450 on the DJIA became support. From left to right, the first arrow represents the first successful test of this support. Buyers at this support level would have been well rewarded. However, in the second half of 2008, the DJIA swiftly broke this support—see second arrow—and continued lower another 30 percent. Sellers anywhere near this break would have been very relieved.

The DJIA would eventually rise back above the resistance price zone 10,450 to 10,850 (but, not without a fight—see the third circle in chart). The third arrow represents a successful test of this now support zone. I remember giving a speech during the last week of September, when this support was being tested, suggesting that the market would find a bottom and rally from there.

Question and answer:

Question: (October 2008) You were right in not getting my equity exposure to target quite yet, the market has done nothing but drop. Lehman has just filed for bankruptcy. How much worse is it going to get, and when should I get some of my excess cash to work?

Answer: The DJIA, currently trading at roughly 8,600, has broken through almost every major support so it is hard to know exactly when the carnage will end. Looking at monthly chart 16.11 of the DJIA, you see a lot of support right around 7,500. The DJIA had dropped to that level on four different occasions and bounced each time. But, it is common for markets to break support temporarily just to rise back above it, so we have to be aware of that. I would start buying in 3 phases. Phase 1 will occur if the market drops to 7,500. If phase 1 occurs, phase 2 will occur if the market drops to 7,000. If phase 1 and 2 occur, I would wait until the DJIA rises back above the 8,000 level. The market should come pretty close to the support areas I mention and if they do, and they bounce from there, that is a good sign that a long-term bottom is in.

Momentum

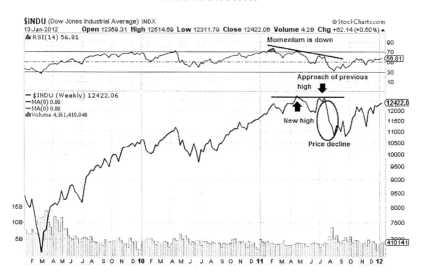

Chart 16.12

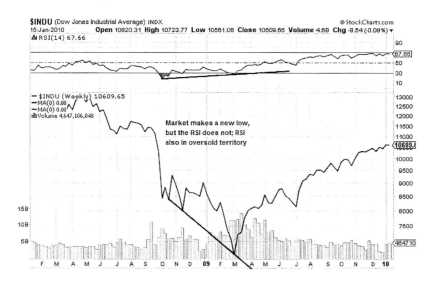

Chart 16.13

A momentum indicator measures the rate of change of prices and is typically shown on a graph as an oscillator that stays within a defined boundary of values. There are many ways to measure momentum such as the relative strength index (RSI), stochastics, and moving average convergence divergence (MACD). However, the measurement that is the easiest to understand and the most useful is the relative strength index. As such the RSI will be the only momentum indicator I will discuss.

> RSI is calculated using the following formula:
> RSI = 100 − [100 / (1 + RS)], where
> RS = (average of x days' up closes) / (average of x days' down closes)

John Murphy (1990, 240) in explaining RSI:

> Fourteen days are used in the calculation; 14 weeks are used in weekly charts. To find the average up value, add the total points gained on up days during the 14 days and divide that total by 14. To find the average down value, add the total number of points lost during the down days and divide that total by 14. Relative strength is then determined by dividing the up average by the down average. That relative strength value is then inserted into the formula for RSI.

If you study the formula carefully, you will see that when the market gains more than it loses over the previous fourteen weeks (fourteen days in the case of daily charts), the RSI value is larger. When the market loses more than it gains during the previous fourteen weeks, the RSI value is smaller. These values are plotted in oscillator format. In chart 16.13, RSI for the DJIA is plotted above its price chart. Because the RSI oscillates, any value above 70 the market is considered to be in overbought territory and any value below 30 is considered to be in oversold territory.

Within the context of broad market analysis, the main benefit of RSI is in identifying positive and negative divergences, which may precede a significant move in the market. A negative divergence occurs when the market makes a new high or reaches a previous high, but the RSI does not. To make this divergence more meaningful, the RSI should be in overbought territory. The idea here is that although the market is making a new high, it is doing so on less and less momentum, suggesting that the market may be running out of steam. Notice in chart 16.12, the DJIA made a new high for the year in April of 2011 and then approached that high again in August. However, the RSI was in overbought territory and made a series of lower highs. The DJIA went on to decline 15 percent over the next couple of months.

A positive divergence occurs when the market makes a new low or reaches a previous low, but the RSI does not. To make this divergence more meaningful, the RSI should be in oversold territory. In chart 16.13, you see the DJIA making a new low in March of 2009, however, RSI did not. Also, RSI was in oversold territory. The DJIA went on to begin a new primary bull market.

The choice of data frequency is an important component of momentum. The longer the time period under analysis—such as weekly or monthly charts—the more significant the divergence in terms of the impending potential primary move in the market. For example, a positive divergence on a monthly chart could portend the start of a new primary market move. A positive divergence on a daily chart on the other hand, would only likely portend a short-lived market rally.

Reversal patterns using Japanese candlesticks

Reversal patterns help to identify turning points in the market's intermediate or primary trend (we discussed intermediate and primary trends in chapter 13). As such, the time frequency used to illustrate these patterns are weekly and monthly charts. Daily charts are of little value in longer term forecasting since they consist of a lot of noise.

Bearish weekly engulfing pattern

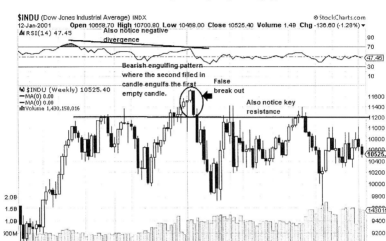

Chart 16.14

A *bearish* engulfing consists of two Japanese candles and occurs when the first white (empty) candle is "engulfed" by the second black (filled) candle. This shows that supply has overwhelmed demand (Nison 2001, 43). In order for the bearish engulfing pattern to have significance it must come after an uptrend and preferably occur at a defined resistance level. Bearish engulfing patterns that appear on weekly or monthly charts can have significant predictive power in determining the end of a primary trend and the start of another primary trend. Chart 16.14 is a weekly chart of the DJIA covering the period surrounding the start of the Tech Wreck and is a good example of the bearish engulfing pattern in action. In January of 2000, the DJIA had a week where it closed well below its open and "wrapped" the positive week prior to it. Notice that this occurred at a key resistance area as defined by a few tests of the previous high. The penetration of this resistance line did not last long, and the bearish engulfing pattern was a sign that this was a false break out. In addition, there was a negative divergence occurring with RSI. For purposes of long-term market forecasting, analysis of engulfing patterns are best used on weekly charts.

Bullish weekly engulfing pattern

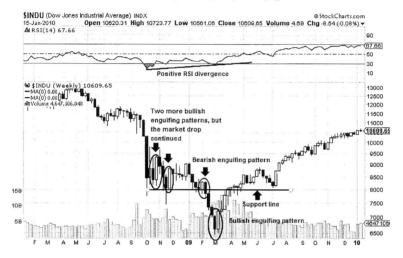

Chart 16.15

The bullish engulfing pattern is the exact opposite of the bearish engulfing pattern and should coincide with a market bottom or support level. Since there is a lot to illustrate in chart 16.15, I will illustrate each annotation from left to right:

- The first arrow shows the first bullish engulfing pattern that occurred in October of 2008. However the market was in a free fall and there was no support level in sight. As such, this bullish engulfing pattern was of little significance.
- The second arrow shows the second bullish engulfing pattern that had occurred in November of 2008. At this

juncture, one would feel pretty good about the possibility that the market was beginning to turn the corner because the support level at DJIA 8,000 had been tested the month before at the previous bullish engulfing pattern. DJIA 8,000 can now be considered a minor support level because it had been successfully tested twice. I typically require more than two successful tests of support before I declare it anything more than of minor importance.

- The third arrow shows the DJIA once again testing this 8,000 level. This is a point of crucial importance. A bounce from this support would be great. A break below this support level would be a concern. Because the cross below occurred with a bearish engulfing pattern, there was clue that the support at 8,000 would be breached and the market would continue lower.

- The fourth circle from the left shows the bullish engulfing pattern that would signify the market's bottom. How did you know that this weekly bullish engulfing pattern would not result in another round of market decline as was the case in the last two? This is a valid question. First notice in chart 16.15 the divergence between price and RSI. This divergence suggests that the market decline was running out of gas. Also, one needed to look at a monthly chart covering the last fifteen years to get a sense of where there could be support. This is how devastating this market drop was.

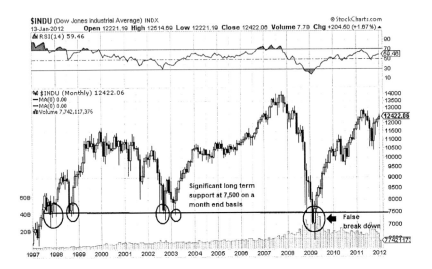

Chart 16.16

Chart 16.16 is a monthly candlestick chart of the DJIA between 1997 and 2012. You can see the significant degree of support at roughly 7,500 using month end data. This level was successfully tested on four different occasions prior to 2009. Now, it has been successfully tested on five different occasions including February 2009. There was a false break down in February of 2009, but March proved to be an exceptionally powerful month that took the DJIA back above support.

Weekly reversals

A concept similar to the bearish and bullish engulfing patterns is called the weekly reversal. In a bearish weekly reversal, you have a week that carried itself above the high of the prior week, but closed below the low of the prior week. In a bullish weekly reversal you have a week that carried itself below the low of the week prior, but closed above the high of the week prior. If these occur at key resistance and support respectively, be careful for a trend reversal in the making.

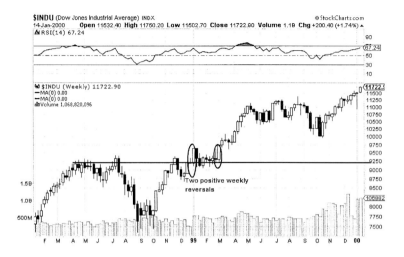

Chart 16.17

The horizontal line in chart 16.17 represents a key resistance and support line. In the first circle, you will see at the tail end of 1998 the DJIA carried itself below the previous weeks low, but closed above the high of the prior week at a significant support level. This is a bullish weekly reversal. Similarly, the DJIA had another bullish reversal week in March of 1999 at the same support level. The weekly reversal is similar in concept to the bullish and bearish engulfing patterns.

Fibonacci retracements

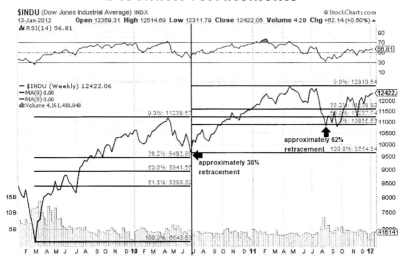

Chart 16.18

No primary uptrend ever continues without some kind of interruption. Similarly, no primary downtrend ever continues without a counter trend rally. When these interruptions occur it is natural to wonder how deep these retracements will be before the prior trend continues. Fibonacci retracements are used for such a purpose. Fibonacci retracement is named after mathematician Leonardo Fibonacci in the thirteenth century. The Fibonacci number sequence is 1, 1, 2, 3, 5, 8, 13, 21, 34, 55, 89, and so on. Each subsequent number in this sequence is the sum of the previous two numbers. Fibonacci numbers have had wide application to many social and natural phenomena. Notice how after number 5, the ratio of a number to its subsequent number approaches .62. For example, 21/34 = .62. As such, the inverse of .62 is .38. The ratios of the Fibonacci sequence before the number 13 are as follows: 1/1 = 100%, ½ = 50%, and 2/3 = 67%. The most common used numbers in retracement analysis are 62%, 38%, and 50%....in a strong trend, a minimum retracement is usually *around* 38%...in a weaker trend, the maximum percentage retracement is usually 62% (Murphy 1999, 336).

Chart 16.18 is a weekly chart of the DJIA that shows the primary bull market that started in March of 2009. In this chart, I have two sets of Fibonacci retracement lines separated by a vertical line. The first set retraces the rally that started in March of 2009 and stalled in May of 2010. Notice the retracement was within 2% of the 38.2% retracement level. The second set of Fibonacci retracement lines retraces the rally that started in June of 2010 and stalled in August of 2011. Notice the retracement was within 1% of the 61.8% retracement level. Because of my preference for using weekly and monthly charts over daily charts, my general rule when using Fibonacci retracements is to give the 38%, 50%, and 62% levels a little leeway. Anything within 2% of each of these levels is equally valid. Because the second major retracement of the primary bull market that began in March of 2009 was deeper than the first suggests that the market may be weakening.

Market Breadth

The most powerful stock market rallies occur when the vast majority of stocks are moving up. What often occurs in the latter phases of a primary bull market is the stock market is propelled by fewer and fewer stocks, which is a sign of pending weakness. When the stock market is declining relentlessly, a bad omen is when the vast majority of stocks are carrying the market lower; this is known as a "take no prisoners" market. However, when a market decline is in its late stages the number of stocks carrying the market lower becomes fewer and fewer, which is a sign of pending strength. Measuring the "health" of a market by comparing the movement of the stock market with its individual constituents is a concept known as market breadth. There are many market breadth indicators, but the only one I find value in for purposes of broad market forecasting is the advance-decline (AD) line.

According to Murphy (1999, 243):

> The advance-decline line tells us whether or not the broader universe of 3500 NYSE stocks is advancing in line with the most widely followed stock averages, which include only the 30 Dow Industrials or the 500 stocks in the S&P 500…to paraphrase a Wall Street maxim: the advance-decline line tells us if the "troops" are keeping up with the "generals"…as long as the AD line is advancing with the Dow Industrials, for example, the breadth or health of the market is good.

The advance-decline line takes the difference between advancing issues and declining issues for the week (or day) and charts this number on a cumulative basis. An extended period of stocks rising over stocks declining results in an AD line that trends up, while an extended period of stocks declining over stocks rising results in an AD line that trends down. Typically the AD line tops out or bottoms before the stock market indexes.

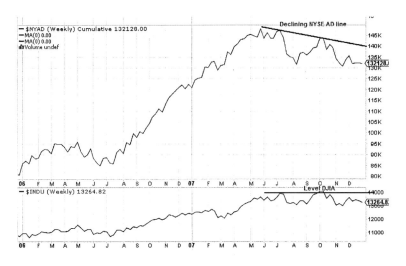

Chart 16.19

Chart 16.19 shows the NYSE Ad line (top) slope downward while the DJIA (bottom) level out at toward the end of 2007.

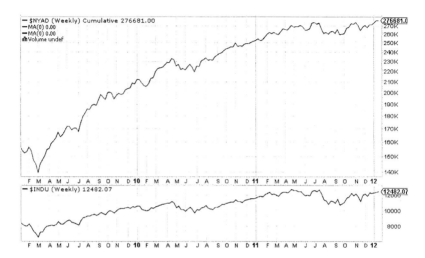

Chart 16.20

Chart 16.20 shows the NYSE Ad line (top) following in sync with the DJIA (bottom), a sign of a healthy market.

Chapter 17

FUNDAMENTAL MARKET VARIABLES

The yield curve

The yield curve is the difference between short-term treasury rates and long-term treasury rates. Some people will use the fed funds rate as the short-term rate and the thirty-year treasury yield for the longer term rate while others will use the two year treasury yield for the short-term rate and the ten year treasury as the long-term rate. However you define yield curve, the concept remains the same: the yield curve has a tendency to take certain shapes at various times in the business cycle.

A normal yield curve occurs when investors are compensated with higher interest rates as the bond maturities extend further out into the future. An acceptable difference between short and long rates to be considered normal is 2%. Any difference greater than 2% is considered a steep yield curve. A flat yield curve, as the name implies, occurs when short-term rates are roughly equal to long-term rates. An inverted yield curve occurs when short-term rates are higher than long-term rates. The transition in the yield curve from normal to flat, from flat to inverted, and inverted to steep has historically coincided with the ups and downs of the business cycle. This makes sense because interest rates are a function of the supply and demand of money, and money is what makes the economy function.

A normal yield curve usually occurs during the regular growth phase of the business cycle. As inflation begins to pick up, the fed begins to raise short-term interest rates to slow down the economy so inflation doesn't get out of hand. Eventually, as a result of so many fed-induced interest rate increases, the yield curve begins to flatten. At this point, because borrowing costs are now higher and money has been taken out of the banking system, the economy begins to slow down. In response, investors will start expecting a slow-down in the economy and begin their "flight to quality" where long-term treasuries are purchased—causing long-term interest rates to drop—and higher risk assets are sold. The combination of higher short rates and a flight to quality causes the yield curve to invert, which has historically been a precursor to the beginning of a recession. The yield curve became inverted in January of 2007. A recession was declared in December of 2007. When the economy is in a recession, the Fed will usually begin a series of short-term interest rate reductions. A result of these short-term interest rate reductions, the yield curve becomes steep, which is symbolic of the Fed's attempt to fight off deflation.

Industrial production

Industrial production is a measure of all the industrial output in the United States. This output number is produced monthly by the Federal Reserve Board and includes mining, utilities, and consumer manufacturing. Industrial production is a coincident indicator meaning that it has a tendency to move in synchronization with the U.S. economy. If industrial production expands too much, there is a tendency for it to exert inflationary pressure as capacity utilization in the economy increases causing manufacturers to pass on higher prices to consumers or engage in investments to expand capacity, both of which are inflationary.

Consumer expectations

The Consumer Confidence Index comes out monthly and is the best measure of consumer expectations. This survey measures a cross sample of consumers across the country to gauge the general "feeling" of consumers. Consumer expectations have a tendency to move in tandem with the direction of the stock market because the media is often a cheerleader for stocks as they are rising and a promoter of negative news as stocks are falling. The media plays an important role in shaping consumer expectations. Because the stock market is a leading indicator, consumer expectations are a leading indicator as well. However, it is not a good idea to sell stocks when consumer expectations are falling because the stock market is also a reflection of risk. When there is a perceived increase in risk throughout the financial system, consumer expectations have a tendency to decline as consumers respond to the negative feedback loop of data created by the media. Many risk-based corrections end quickly just to have the longer term primary uptrend continue. Because risk-based corrections occur frequently, investors will get whipsawed trying to sell every time the Consumer Confidence Index drops and buying when it goes up. The Consumer Confidence Index can be volatile from month to month because consumer expectations are very fickle.

Interest rates

Interest rates are determined by the supply and demand for credit as discussed in chapter 7. When the Federal Reserve increases interest rates, credit is harder to obtain and less attractive to borrow. When the Federal Reserve reduces interest rates, credit is easier to obtain and more attractive to borrow. The direction of interest rates is an important component of the economy and plays a significant role going into recessions and coming out of recessions.

The four stages of an economic cycle

The four fundamental variables just discussed—yield curve, industrial production, consumer expectations, and interest rates—have a tendency to exhibit certain characteristics within the economic cycle. The economic cycle can be broken down into four stages. The stages, in order, are early recovery, full recovery, early recession, and full recession. Following is a summary of Sam Stovall's sector rotation model, which indicates the following characteristics associated with each stage:

Early recovery–Early recoveries are typically associated with: 1) rising consumer expectations 2) rising industrial production 3) bottoming interest rates 4) normal to steep yield curve.
Full recovery – Full recoveries are typically associated with: 1) falling consumer expectations 2) flat industrial production 3) rates rising rapidly 4) flattening out yield curve
Early recession – Early recessions are typically associated with: 1) consumer expectations falling sharply 2) falling industrial production 3) peaking interest rates 4) flat or inverted yield curve
Full recession – Full recessions are typically associated with: 1) reviving consumer expectations 2) bottoming industrial production 3) falling interest rates 4) normal yield curve[22]

If you can identify which stage of the economic cycle we are in, then you will know which stage is next and therefore be able to position your financial portfolio accordingly knowing that the market always leads the economic cycle.

Credit spreads

Although credit spreads are not part of Stovall's theoretical model, they are still an important part of understanding the financial markets. Although there are many credit "spreads," the only one that concerns us for purposes of broad market and economic forecasting is the spread between high yield bonds and a risk-free treasury. The spread is the difference in yield between these two investment instruments. A high yield bond is a debt instrument issued by a low credit-quality issuer and is considered much riskier than a treasury bond of comparable maturity. A larger spread means high yield bonds are being sold off, treasuries are being purchased, or a combination of both. Spreads become wide during periods of "high risk" or perceived high risk.

Where I find value in credit spreads is when the market is correcting because of some kind of risk related to the financial system or maybe a sovereign default, but credit spreads are relatively contained. In this scenario, the market is going down because of fear, but the bond market (the high yield to treasury credit spread) suggests that this fear may be overblown. For example, in August and September of 2011, the DJIA dropped in excess of 15% because of fear related to the debacle in Greece and the potential for sovereign defaults to spread to Italy and Spain, a scenario that would have reaped havoc on the seventeen-country European Union that all share the euro as their common currency. However, high yield to treasury credit spreads were the same as they were in early 2010 when there was little concern regarding Greece's potential sovereign default.

Chapter 18

RATE OF CHANGE

When it comes to profiting in the financial markets, regardless if it is the stock market, commodity market, or fixed income market, it is important not to get caught up on the *absolute* level of misery in a declining market or *absolute* level of optimism in a market that is going up. In a market that is declining, ask yourself are things likely to get worse at a *faster or slower rate of change* relative to the rate of change of the past six to nine months. Similarly, in a market that is going up, ask yourself are things likely to get better at a *faster or slower rate* relative to the past six to nine months. Having some knowledge of the social-political and economic environment and their effect on the actions of businesses, consumers, government, the Fed, and investors is a vital component in answering the question about the future rate of change of the economy.

The DJIA bottomed in March of 2009 and began a spectacular primary bull market. However, the economy's recession was not declared over until six months later in August of 2009. Why did the market begin to go up six months prior to the end of the recession? The answer is because the stock market anticipated that the rate of declining growth was slowing. Investors are all looking for "the next best thing" and therefore they try to anticipate when a big move in the market is about to occur before the fundamentals get obviously better. Investment capital always moves before significant changes in the fundamentals.

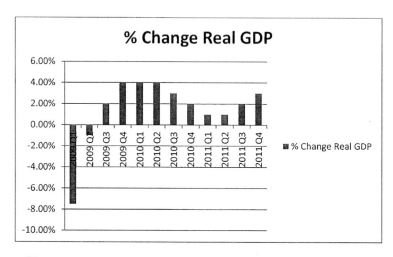

Chart 18.1

Chart 18.1 shows the seasonally adjusted rate of quarterly change in real gross domestic product (GDP), notice in 2009, the first quarter had a drop in GDP of nearly 8%. However, the second quarter's decline was much less (although still negative). Finally in the third quarter the *slowing rate of decline* led to a positive change in real GDP. The stock market anticipated this slowing rate of decline six months earlier and commenced what would be the beginning of a primary bull market.

In practice it is difficult to anticipate what the future rate of change in the economy is going to be. This difficulty is compounded by the fact that the media will always make you believe things will get worse during a primary bear market and make you believe things will always get better during a primary bull market. But the concepts learned in part 2 "Understanding the Current Environment" will help shed a more objective light on what is really happening. Because the market leads the economy, the concepts learned in part 3 "Understanding Market Behavior" will also help shed some light on what the market is saying about the future direction of the economy. The strongest convictions occur when the conclusion about the current environment are in synch with what the market is saying about the macro environment.

A thorough study of history also illustrates the importance of understanding the rate in which change happens. *Investors are quick to grasp on to concepts that can change the world without giving much thought to the rate and speed in which it takes for these concepts to make a material difference for the benefit of society.* The risk is that investors will be extremely early or late to the game. A constant theme after the Financial Collapse of 2008 as I met with clients was concern about the United States debt load. The United States debt load approaching 100% of GDP and likely rising above that in the years to come is a very serious matter as the interest component of the debt rises to alarming levels. Without a corresponding increase in productivity so that GDP can rise to compensate for this increasing debt load, our debt will become less and less attractive to foreign financiers. However, the adjustment process and therefore the economic ramifications of a slow-down in spending, a reduced reliance on foreign financing, an increased reliance on domestic saving, and balancing between tax incentives and entitlement programs is a process that will take decades to complete. Meanwhile there will be plenty of primary bull markets to benefit from. Going from the most economically productive and militaristically powerful country in the world to a sudden liquidity crisis such as what occurred in Greece in 2011 is not going to happen, let alone happen overnight. The point is, don't let yourself get caught up in assuming the *rate of change* of this adjustment process is going to happen within a short time frame. Similarly, investors in the highly touted nanotechnology stocks in 2004 failed to appreciate the length of time it takes for a disruptive technology to gain consumer acceptance and commercial viability. For example, it took household electricity and the telephone 46 and 33 years respectively to reach 25% of the population. Nanotechnology still has a long way to go to be commercially viable. In addition, for the six weeks ended

September 2012 stocks in the eurozone were up an astonishing 15 percent. At the beginning of October, I read the following headline, "eurozone manufacturing production declined for the seventh month running in September, however the *rate of contraction* eased to a five-month low."

The main point behind the concept of rate of change is simply to understand that it is not the current situation in *absolute* terms that dictates what the market is going to do; it is the anticipation, or rate of change, that the market cares the most about. When things are falling apart and the world is full of flaws, ask what can go right. When things are great and the world is full of stars, ask yourself what can go wrong.

Question and answer

Question: I am glad I took that Calculus course in college because I understand now the rate of change. Can you give me an example of how the concept of rate of change can help me make better investment decisions?

Answer: Banking and credit conditions will improve significantly in 2012. The velocity of money has been low for a long time because people aren't transacting like they used to. But real estate is showing signs of a bottom, and housing affordability is at an all-time high meaning that relative to income housing is more affordable now than it has been in the last two decades. As a result banks are seeing support for housing prices. This will give banks the confidence to lend again. In fact, I believe this is occurring right now. The rate of change of economic activity should pick up as a result; therefore the stock market should have a good year as well.

Part 4
Strategy and Discipline

Strategy and Discipline 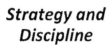 Understanding your goals and objectives

Understanding market behavior

Understanding the current macro environment

Chapter 19

STRATEGIES

Direction of trend – risk on or risk off

Once you have developed an understanding of your own unique financial goals, engaged in the critical thinking process of understanding the sociopolitical and economic environment, and have a sense of how the market will behave in such environments, the next step is to establish a tactical investment strategy. *The biggest decision to make when developing a tactical investment strategy is whether to be on offense or defense. This is known as the "risk-on" or "risk-off" strategy respectively.* If, after a thorough assessment of the market and its environment, you feel that the market is headed for a sustained primary bull market, you will want to be on offense or engage in risk-on strategies. On the other hand, if you believe that the market is headed for a sustained primary bear market, you will want to be on defense or engage in risk-off strategies. As you read through this part of the book on investment strategies, I recommend that you refer back to chapter 16 on technical analysis because many of the entry and exit strategies discussed here are based on these technical methodological tools.

Trend

The first step in determining your strategy is deciding on what trend is taking place in the market. The market always has to be in one of four phases: 1) trending, either up or down 2) accumulation by long-term investors 3) Distribution by long-term investors 4) Consolidating sideways (Sperandeo 1993, 54). We've discussed two levels of trend in chapter 13, the primary trend and the intermediate trend. The primary trend is the longer trend of the market and is defined as a move that takes the market 20% above or below the current level *and* takes at least twelve months to form. These are the important trends that you want to be prepared for. The intermediate trend is shorter than the primary trend and can last a few weeks to a few months. The intermediate trend unfolds within the primary trend and is usually short-lived. Very rarely does an intermediate trend carry the market more than 15% in the direction counter to the primary trend. For example, in a primary bull market trend, seldom does the intermediate counter trend bring the market down more than 15%. In a primary bear market trend, it is uncommon that the intermediate trend bring the market up more than 15%. All the tools and methods discussed in parts 2 and 3 of this book will help you determine the direction of trend for the market. Once you have determined the primary or intermediate trend of the market and whether you want to put risk on or take risk off, the next question becomes a matter of logistics. At *what* price level for the market do you begin to initiate or eliminate positions? *When* do you begin to initiate or eliminate positions? What triggers need to happen before you start implementation of portfolio rebalancing? Answering these logistical questions is the purpose of Part 4.

If you want to be more aggressive in your tactical investment strategy, you can try and time the intermediate term trends. Of course, timing these intermediate term trends carries a heightened degree of risk because they are more difficult to time. On the other hand, if you are more concerned with being a head of the longer term primary trend, then identifying when such trends may start, end, or continue are the more important considerations. Typically, I recommend that investors focus more attention on longer primary trends; however, I would not hesitate to be more aggressive in timing the intermediate term trends if I felt strongly enough about their development. I don't make any attempt to time the hourly and daily trends of the market because the margin for error in day-trading is too high and the benefit is not worth the time and energy involved.

Question and answer:

Question: I have heard a lot lately about gold, but it has been trending so strongly I hate to buy it at this price. What are your thoughts?

Answer: I think globalization and the rapid movement of capital across borders has created so much efficiency and productivity the past forty years that inflation has not really taken over as many of the gold bugs would want to believe. We have been off any form of gold standard now for over forty years, which is the longest stretch of time in history where gold has not played a role in our monetary system. Who knows if we could have achieved the spectacular growth and productivity in the world if we were still on the gold standard.

Gold is priced too high given it has no importance as a monetary anchor. However, the trend is very strong. Even when the price of gold corrects, it does so mildly. There just isn't that sense that gold wants to drop in value significantly any time soon. Since it is at an all-time high, it is hard to forecast when the resistance areas will be.

At this point, the trend in gold is so strong, I have to assume that it will continue to go up. Retail investors will bid up the metal to new heights, and the big players will sell right into it. When it drops, it will drop big. In sum, because the trend is so strong, you should have a tactical allocation to gold; however, be ready to reduce or eliminate your position if major support levels are broken.

Now that you have an understanding of the sociopolitical and economic environment, an understanding of how the market may behave in such environments, and based on this understanding you have determined the primary direction of the market, you must choose a strategy that will best accomplish your objectives. I will discuss some of the strategies that have been useful for me in my career. Regardless of the chosen strategy, it is always good practice to implement offensive and defensive market strategies in phases. In other words, if you are on offense never buy into your desired allocation to the stock market all at once. If you are on defense, never reduce your stock market allocation to your desired level all at once. I find that the magical number 3 is generally a good rule of thumb when positioning offensively or defensively. When you want to be on offensive because you think the primary trend will be up, then buy in 3 phases. If you want to be on defense because you think the primary trend will be down then sell in 3 phases. *The last thing I will mention about strategies is to always have one. Always be one step ahead of the market by knowing what you are going to do next.*

Price strategies

Rules based on price operate on the premise that the price level will determine entry and exit points. If you are on offense and believe that the market direction is up, you want to be a buyer of the market. Here you must determine at which price level or levels you will enter the market. When determining these levels, you must have entry points that are above as well as below the current market. The reason for having entry points above the market is due to the possibility that the market may not drop to your pre-determined level. In this case you do not want to be sitting on the sidelines if you have already determined that you want to be in the market.

On the other hand, if you are on defense and believe that the market direction is down, you want to be a seller of the market. Here you must determine at which price level or levels you will exit the market. When determining these levels, you must have exit points that are below as well as above the market. The reason for having exit points below the market is because of the possibility that the market may not rise to your pre-determined level, in which case you don't want to be sitting on an overabundance of risky assets if you have determined that there is potential for a primary bear market to be unfolding. Do nothing until either of these price levels is reached. Knowing these levels and already have given thought to them will enable you to reduce emotions and be patient.

Point strategies

A close relative to the price strategy is what I call the point strategy. The idea is pretty simple. If you are a buyer of the market (if you think the primary trend is going to be up) you will wait for the market to drop a certain number of points before you begin implementing your strategy of getting into the market. On the other hand, if you are a seller of the market (if you think the primary trend is going to be down), you will wait until the market goes up a certain number of points before you begin implementing your strategy of getting out of the market.

Similar to the price level strategy discussed earlier, you must have a point strategy above and below the market. For example, if the DJIA is trading at a level of 10,000 and you think the primary trend is going to be down and you elect a point strategy, you will need to determine the number of points above and below the market in which you will begin selling your stocks. Let's say you elect 250 Dow points as your trigger mechanism. This means if the DJIA goes up to 10,250 or down to 9,750, you will begin your selling strategy. Once these levels are hit, perform the first phase of your risk reduction. In this example, let's say the market does indeed go up to your desired 10,250 level. What next? Now, you use your same 250 point strategy and apply it to DJIA 10,250. If the DJIA goes up to 10,500 or back down to 10,000, you will implement your second phase of risk reduction. Continue on this path until your three phases are complete.

In volatile markets I like to start with larger point drop or gain, such as 500 Dow points. In less volatile markets I like to start with smaller point drop or gains, such as 250 points. There is nothing magical about these numbers. In reality you will want to adjust them up or down depending on what is trying to be accomplished and general market conditions that prevail at that time. Another strategy could also be using a combination of 500 or 250 points. For example, if you believe the market will be volatile at first, but will settle down a bit after a large point move, then start with 500 points as your initial trigger and then drop it to 250 points for the second and third phases.

Question and answer

Question: In November 2008 the market was extremely volatile, and I wasn't sure I wanted to even think about buying into the stock market. But if I did, what strategy would you recommend?

Answer: I would use a combination of a price level and point strategy. After Lehman Brothers filed for bankruptcy, the DJIA was trading at 8,000. There was a lot of support on a monthly 15-year chart at around 7,500. I would begin buying if the DJIA drops to 7,500. At the rate the market had been dropping, I was pretty certain this target will be hit. However, if it was not hit and the market experienced a sustained rebound without ever dropping to 7,500, we would need another entry point. There is some resistance at 8,500. The downtrend line—achieved by connecting the lower highs of the previous several months—would be broken to the upside at approximately DJIA 8,500. If the market went up to 8,500 before it hit 7,500, we would use that price level to begin buying in. Once these levels were reached, I would buy in again using a point strategy of 500 points. For example, if the market dropped to 7,500, the next buy in would occur at 8,000 or 7,000. The last of the three-phase offensive strategy, I would use a point strategy of 250 points.

Momentum strategies

Rules based on momentum (see chapter 16) are based on the simple premise that overbought and oversold conditions will determine entry and exit points. If you want to be on offense and want to be a buyer of the market, wait until oversold conditions exist. But have an alternative strategy if the oversold conditions are not met. If you want to be on defense and want to be a seller of the market, wait until overbought conditions exist. But also have a sell strategy in case the overbought condition does not occur. If your oversold (if you are on offense) and overbought (if you are on defense) conditions are not met and you need a strategy to help implement your tactical investment plan, consider one of the other rules bases strategies discussed in this section in conjunction with the technical analysis tools discussed in Part 3 of this book. For example, if you are looking to be defensive in your strategy and your initial inclination is to wait for an overbought market but you want to have a plan B in case your overbought conditions are not met, you can use a price based strategy that uses key support levels as the levels where you will exit the market.

Time strategies

Rules based on time are probably the simplest of the rules based strategies. Time strategies dictate when you will make portfolio rebalancing trades in the direction you believe the market will go. If you believe the primary trend is down, for example, you will begin reducing risk. If you believe the primary trend is up, you will begin increasing risk. The first step in timing strategies is to determine *the total length of time* it will take your strategy to be fully complete. For example, if you are a buyer of the market, you may want to be fully allocated to your risk exposure over a four (any number will do) month period. The second step in timing strategies is to determine the *frequency* of your rebalancing trades. Time strategies are a dollar-cost-averaging strategy, where you move into or out of the market over a certain period of time at predetermined frequencies. For example, if you are a seller of the market, you may want to be at your target risk exposure by selling equities once a month for four months at the exact same time each month. The benefit of time strategies is that they are automatic as they take the emotion and "guessing" game out of the decision making process.

Question and answer

Question: In January 2011 I sold one of my houses and had all this cash. How would you suggest I invest it?

Answer: When it comes to investing, timing and strategy is everything. In an election year typically the year's gains are concentrated in the second half of the year. January looked like it would end on a very good note. It was doubtful that February, March, April, May, and June would experience the same returns as January. That is just not sustainable. I recommend that we buy into the market in 1/5 increments, starting now with the first tranche. Then, we would do the exact same thing one month from then and continue until we were fully allocated in June. This would allow us to take advantage of the volatility that I expected to occur between then and June.

Sentiment strategies

During fundamentally difficult sociopolitical and economic environments, a good money-making strategy is to go opposite the retail investor. In this sense, sentiment strategies are similar to momentum strategies. Overbought markets typically coincide with positive retail sentiment, and oversold markets typically coincide with negative retail sentiment. Sentiment is the degree of optimism or pessimism displayed by retail investors in aggregate. In using sentiment strategies, you will want to sell when there is an overabundance of optimism and buy when there is an overabundance of pessimism. There are various ways to measure sentiment. For example, you can measure sentiment through put-call ratios, high yield to treasury yield spread, Rydex Nova/Ursa ratio, American Association of Individual Investors (AAII) survey, etc. My preference is to use the AAII website that publishes weekly the results of their survey. According to Shell Capital Management in their article *Asymmetric Investment Returns*:

> The AAII Sentiment Survey measures the percentage of individuals who are bullish, bearish, and neutral about the stock market over the next six months. Originally started in 1987 as a weekly survey sent out via snail mail to a random sample of AAII members, the survey has been conducted on-line since the beginning of 2000. Members of AAII can vote once a week at the Member Surveys area of AAII.com. Results of the survey are compiled on a weekly basis (Thursdays) at the AAII Web site and are also published weekly in Barron's. The average AAII member is a male in his late-50s with a graduate degree. In addition, over half of AAII members have an investment portfolio of at least $500,000. Taking this into account, the AAII Sentiment Survey is unique among sentiment surveys in

that it represents the upper echelon of active, hands-on individual investors.[23]

There are two ways to use the AAII Sentiment Survey. First you can measure the rate of change of those who are bullish or bearish on the market. Secondly, you can use the absolute value of those who are bullish or bearish on the market.

When using the rate of change, you will want to begin a risk off strategy when the rate of change of those surveyed that are bullish increases by 50% or more or begin a risk on strategy when the rate of change of those that are bullish decreases by 50% or more over a two to three week period. There is nothing special about the 50% rate of change. This is just a rate of change that I have found effective. However, one can adjust this to best fit with the environment at hand. Using the rate of change of the AAII bullish survey is best used in a trendless market.

When using the absolute value of the AAII Sentiment Survey, you can begin a risk off strategy when the level of bullishness reaches 70% or begin a risk on strategy when the level of bullishness reaches 25%. Using absolute percentages in this fashion is best used in a market that is trending either up or down respectively.

Question and answer:

Question: I was frustrated with the volatility of the market in July 2010. It seems like every time something good is happening the market drops and when something horrible is happening the market goes up. What should I do?

Answer: You should take advantage of this volatility. This is a fundamentally difficult environment. Yes, the economy is marginally getting better. But, you still have a depressed housing market and significant concerns in Europe. I track a sentiment survey and when retail investors as a group have a significant jump in optimism the market sells off. When retail investors as a group have a significant drop in optimism the market goes up.

One interesting note is that, despite the market going up nearly 70% from the low that was set in March of 2009, the absolute level of optimists never exceeded 51%. The market has gone up 70% while retail investors have sat on the sideline! So here is our strategy, when the rate of change of optimism goes up by 50% or more—meaning people who are optimistic that the market will go up over the next six months goes up by 50% or more—consider rebalancing and taking gains. When the rate of change of optimism goes down by 30–50% or more—meaning people who are pessimistic about the market goes up by 30–50% or more—consider buying into the market. Eventually, however, investors will catch on to this trend and the evolution of optimism to pessimism. When the absolute level of optimism breaks above 51%, we should abandon this strategy because that means the market may be in store for a sustainable rise, right when retail investors least expect it.

Chapter 20

IMPLEMENTATION: THE IMPORTANCE OF DISCIPLINE

No matter how smart, knowledgeable, educated, or experienced you are, if you do not have the discipline and emotional fortitude to allow yourself to think in different ways and to do the uncomfortable, then you will not succeed in investing in fundamentally difficult environments. The best way to fail in investing is to be emotional and impatient. Markets are built so that the average retail investor, if left to their own devices, will fail. Most of the investing public thinks like investors but act like traders because they constantly allow themselves to become emotional and to be swayed by the media.

Being disciplined involves engaging in those behaviors that result in investment decisions that, when applied systematically and consistently over long periods of time, will stack the odds in your favor to achieve investment success. To engage in those behaviors one must have the mind-set and the ability to think in different, and oftentimes uncomfortable, ways. Understanding the sociopolitical and economic environment, understanding market behavior, having a market-focused investment strategy, and having the emotional discipline to implement your strategy all provide a foundation that will increase your confidence level and therefore increase your ability to make the right decisions when it is most difficult to do so.

A rude awakening

On the flight back to Phoenix from Gainesville, Florida, after having just finished my MBA from the University of Florida, I remember thinking to myself how awful and depressed I felt. My MBA capped eight straight years of continuous post undergraduate education. First I managed to obtain the Chartered Financial Analyst designation in the three years, followed by the Chartered Market Technician in two years, and my MBA in three years, all while working full time. Despite being educated, I felt physically and emotionally drained. I was about fifteen pounds overweight, I had no energy, and constantly second guessing myself. It was that moment on the flight home that I told myself that from now on, I would focus on my physical and emotional self because I knew that to be a successful investment manager I needed much more than experience and education. I needed clarity and focus.

I started a regular exercise and nutrition program. Health and wellness is now a part of my everyday life. Being healthy physically and emotionally has helped me tremendously to deal with the stress associated with the uncertainty of the market. Knowing when to change course in your tactical investment strategy, and just as important, when not to change course requires a great deal of discipline, which is dependent on having clarity and focus. For me, as an investment manager, I have to be ten times more emotionally stable than the average investor because I have to make up for the emotion of all my clients. The market is major source of temptation. Wanting to sell out of fear when the market is dropping, buy out of greed as the market is going up, second guessing yourself after a position has been taken, always allowing yourself to be easily swayed in the direction opposite what you believe, letting pre-conceived opinions and experiences convince you to make a bad investment decision, and not staying the course when you know you should. Having a strong emotional fortitude gives you clarity and focus to sort out the noise of the market and focus on what matters.

To make the process of making disciplined investment decisions easier, I will conclude this book with a set of investing principles that when read and re-read will cause you to re-think your traditional, potentially haphazard way of making investment decisions, and allow you to re-wire your brain's circuitry so that you can win in this fundamentally challenging investment environment. Every great performer—musicians, heart surgeons, dancers, FBI agents, athletes, and leaders—instinctively understands the power of making key behaviors automatic; this is especially valuable under pressure, when fear tends to undermine performance if our skills aren't deeply ritualized (Schwartz 2010, 37).

Investing principles

#1 Do whatever it takes to take the emotion of fear and greed out of the decision making process

- *Objectivity can never be achieved out of fear and greed unless by luck.*

#2 Don't waste valuable energy trying to time the daily and weekly moves in the market; for most people, that is a fool's game

- *Short-term market timing is never worth the energy that is put into it.*

#3 Understand your goals and objectives, understand the macro environment, understand how the market may react in this environment, have a strategy, and have the discipline to implement your strategy

- *Have a process that makes sense*

#4   Only take a position with an attractive reward/risk ratio

- *What is the point if the reward is not greater than the risk?*

#5   Don't put yourself in a desperate situation

- *Never rely on unreasonable returns to meet your income needs.*

#6   Plan your investments and invest your plan

- *Process, strategy, and discipline are important components to investing*

#7   Build up or build down a market position as opposed to doing it all at once. In other words, if you want to position your portfolio defensively expecting a sustained market decline, reduce risk in phases. If you want to position your portfolio offensively expecting a sustained rise, increase risk in phases.

- *You can never consistently time the market just right. Stop trying.*

#8   Always error on the side of being patient

- *When does anything good in life ever occur because of impatience?*

#9   Have a historical perspective

- *Fear repeats, greed repeats, the need for security repeats, short-term sacrifices are rarely made for the benefit of the longer term, and politics will always be politics*

#10 Don't rationalize your emotions once your strategy and plan have been set.

- *Have you ever met people who always seem to be stricken by bad luck? This is why.*

#11 Always have an exit and an entry strategy.

- *Be proactive, not reactive*

#12 Do not disconnect investment decisions from the broader context of the market and the economy

- *The direction of the market dictates all*

#13 Have an international perspective

- *Globalization baby!*

#14 Be absolutely confident about your investment decisions unless the market proves you wrong, and when it does, don't argue

- *A big part of success in any endeavor is knowing when to cut your losses*

#15 Stay in good physical and mental shape. This helps you to stay focused and balances out negative emotions

- *Focus, focus, focus*

#16 Have a long-term view (even if you are 85)

- *It all starts with a long-term view and works backwards*

#17 Think in terms of reactions to events/news especially at key support and resistance levels

- *Reaction to news is always more important than the news*

#18 Don't hope to get lucky

- *Hoping to get lucky is an amateur's game*

#19 At major tops and bottoms, the media is your worst enemy

- *Successful investors know this, and so should you*

#20 Introspection—know your own weaknesses

- *If you are a know-it-all, you are in the wrong business.*

#21 Avoid refusing to sell for a loss if it is the right thing to do

- *Sometimes the best way to make money is to not lose so much of it*

#22 Markets can be manipulated in the short to intermediate term, but in the long run, what should happen does happen

- *The market sometimes has a law of its own that can seem disconnected from what "should" occur. Understand this law.*

#22 Don't throw good money after bad. If you made a bad investment don't "double-down" in a desperate attempt to make you whole

- *When you feel tempted to do this, remember there is always a better place for your money*

#23 Don't be a " long-term investor" if you want to day trade

- *Don't have an identity crisis*

#24 Don't be a "day trader" if you want to be a long-term investor

- *Don't have an identity crisis*

#25 Don't try to outsmart yourself

- *This is what the market wants you to do. Don't fall into its trap.*

#26 Don't throw good energy away by focusing on things that don't make a difference

- *Maximize output per unit of energy*

#27 If you don't own your failures, if you try to blame your failures on outside events, then you will end up not learning from your prior mistakes, and likely end up miserable

- *Man up!*

#28 Don't think about how much money you will make or how much money you will lose

- *Never put the cart before the horse*

#29 Think in terms of equilibriums

- *Focus on what matters*

#30 Think in terms of rate of change because that is where the rubber meets the road in terms of the economy's relation to the stock market

- *Figure out the direction, then figure out the rate of change…one is no good without the other*

#31 Sometimes the best way to make money is not to lose it

- *A 20 percent loss requires a 25 percent gain to return to even. Capisce?*

#32 Be humble! The market is like mother nature; it can destroy you if you become reckless

- *Overconfidence is a killer!*

#33 Define your time frame before you invest

- *Distance = Rate x Time, how are you supposed to know how far and how fast you need to go if you don't know how long you have to get there*

#34 The only certainty is change itself

- *The sooner you come to grips with this, the better*

#35 The correct determination of the direction of the long-term primary trend is the most important factor in investing

- *Don't fight the fundamentals*

#36 You can't get something for nothing

- *To make money, you have to work hard*

#37 Sense opportunity when others see contradiction; chaos and confusion are critical elements of success

- *When one door closes, another door opens*

#38 Diversify, diversify, diversify

- *To diversify is to know what you don't know*

#39 No fear, no ego, no anger

- *Don't make emotional decisions*

#40 Always know what your next plan of action is going to be. Always have a strategy.

- *Take control of the market,*

#41 Avoid tickeritis. In other words, don't spend all day watching CNBC.

- *This is what separates the wealthy from the really wealthy*

#42 Be a life-long learner

- *Now is not the time to stop improving*

Summary of key points

Throughout this book, I have emphasized key points that are integral to remember as you embark on your journey through Wall Street. I have summarized these key points below to serve as a handy reference:

- There is no algorithmic formula or system that will make you an automatic winner at investing in the stock market. If you are willing to put in the time, discipline, and dedication to learning and understanding the market, this book will be an indispensable tool to help guide you in the right direction and stack the odds in your favor.
- Planning your investment is the most important part of the investment and wealth structuring process because it provides the context in which all other key decisions are made.
- Without the proper context, one may fall into the trap of systematically making high risk decisions that eventually will lead to that one fatal financial mistake.

- Whether it be a result of procrastination or skepticism about the process, one should not allow chance to direct their financial future.
- The four most important planning considerations are cash flow, liquidity, growth, and risk management.
- Investing in the stock market is a race to figure out what consumers, investors, businesses, policy makers, and financial intermediaries are going to do next and invest in advance of these actions.
- Don't mistake being informed for being knowledgeable. Information turns into knowledge only when you can use that information for profit.
- The objective of any investment strategy should be based on obtaining a clearer understanding of market dynamics, the sociopolitical and economic environment, and a systemic rewiring of how investment decisions are made.
- What is important is investing for the time frame that is unique and important to you.
- Contrarian is the act of doing something inherently uncomfortable.
- Day trading is a waste of time and valuable energy.
- A forty-year trend toward ever-greater specialization is slowly reversing, forcing investment managers to take on more difficult responsibilities.
- A broad understanding of the interplay between society, politics, and economics serves as the domain in which markets operate, and without a thorough understanding of them, it is extremely difficult to obtain the perspective necessary to achieve long-term investment success.
- The main drivers of all economic activity are consumers, businesses, government, investors, and financial intermediaries.

- Investors need to be careful about assuming that today's events are going to transpire exactly like they had in the past.
- Politics will always be politics, fear will always be fear, greed will always be greed, people will always be impatient, short-term sacrifices are rarely made for the benefit of the longer term, and people and states will always have a need for security.
- History helps one to understand how sociopolitical conditions may take shape given a reference point in which to craft these conclusions from.
- Equilibrium means that no economic actor has an incentive to change his or her behavior and the costs and benefits of the existing situation are judged to have achieved the best balance that an individual could reasonably expect.
- It is better for investors to understand the "feel" of the process of equilibrium formation and to not get bogged down in the details of the specifically defining the precise point of equilibrium.
- The dollar is still the world's defacto currency.
- Gold no longer has a purpose as a monetary anchor.
- The process that we know of as "printing money" occurs through the commercial banking system and is done through the creation of credit.
- Institutional changes based on new ideas and the discrediting of old ideas is a time consuming and politically heated process that usually takes years and sometimes decades to complete.
- Taxation, fiscal soundness, health care, inflation, regulation, deregulation, etc. are all weapons that politicians use to stimulate anger and anxiety among the populace to create coalitions to further their own agenda and to put them on top of the power struggle.

- The fundamentals always win in the long run but can be distorted in the short and intermediate terms.
- By understanding the market's peculiar behavior, you will begin to feel the gap between this behavior and the sociopolitical and economic environment begin to close.
- Mass investor psychology causes extreme values in stocks.
- To take advantage of the inefficiencies of the market in an attempt to beat it requires understanding how the market works and the involvement that human emotion plays in that process.
- Patience is a virtue!
- Most people think their philosophies and views work in every single sociopolitical context; it takes a real thinker to admit that in some contexts their philosophies just don't work.
- We should all be aware of our self-awareness and aware of the lack of self-awareness of others and how that lack of self-awareness, if widespread, can affect consumer and investment decisions.
- Honesty in the absence of compassion becomes cruelty. Tenacity unmediated by flexibility congeals into rigidity. Confidence untempered by humility is arrogance. Courage without prudence is recklessness. Because all virtues are connected to others, any strength overused ultimately becomes a liability.
- The market has a law of its own, and the media's involvement in that law oftentimes seems like a plot against the retail investor to take advantage of the frailties of fear and greed.
- Investors are quick to grasp on to concepts that can change the world without giving much thought to the rate and speed in which it takes for these concepts to make a material difference for the benefit of society.

- The biggest decision to make when developing a tactical investment strategy is whether to be on offense or defense. This is known as the "risk on" or "risk off" strategy respectively.
- Always have a strategy. Remain one step ahead of the market by knowing what you are going to do next.
- The single biggest determinant of investing failure among the investing public is making emotional decisions.
- If hiring an investment professional will help you avoid making detrimental investment decisions, then that is what you need to do.
- The four most important things when hiring any service professional advisor that you will see on a regular basis are trust, service, expertise, and likeability.
- Money should only be a means and never an end it itself.

Chapter 21

HIRING SOMEBODY

You will notice that the first principal under investing principals in the previous chapter is to do whatever it takes to remove the emotion out of the decision making process. Having advised thousands of clients and sat through countless meetings, I know *the single biggest determinant of investing failure among the investing public is making emotional decisions*, which means being greedy at the wrong time or being overly fearful at the wrong time. A worse scenario would be to ignore your investments completely. It is extremely difficult to avoid being gripped by fear and greed because money is an emotional topic and the media is a big promoter of these detrimental feelings. *If hiring an investment professional will help you avoid making detrimental investment decisions, then that is what you should do.*

The last thirty-five years have been characterized by discount and online brokerage companies like Charles Schwab, Ameritrade, E-trade, Vanguard, and Fidelity. Although these companies invented the "do-it-yourself" investor, they have evolved to now provide investment advice to their clients, but, their roots still lie in providing discount brokerage services. Because online trading has worked out so well during a fantasy period of exponential growth, many investors have a false sense of how investing in financial markets actually works. Rather than admit the benefit of working with an advisor, people would rather do nothing because doing nothing is the comfortable thing to do. It is also the wrong thing to do. But hiring the right advisor is not the easiest thing to do. I will elaborate on the most common forms of advisor-client relationships and some of the key issues that underlie the selection process.

Commissions vs. asset-based pricing

A commission-based financial arrangement is where customers are charged a transaction fee every time a buy or sell trade is placed. An asset-based arrangement is one where customers are charged an annual percentage of their total portfolio. Common asset-based arrangements start at 1.25 percent and then go down from there depending on the total portfolio size under management. My preference is for an asset-based arrangement because there is an alignment between advisor and client. The more money the advisor makes for you, the more money the advisor makes because the fee is based on a percentage of assets-under-management. With a commission-based arrangement, it is difficult to tell if your advisor is making a recommendation because it is in the best interest of your financial portfolio or if it is in his or her best interest.

Financial planners

Some industry practitioners hang their hat on doing only financial planning but charge an annual fee based on assets "under management" or charge a "product" fee depending on what they sell you. Here the financial planner will engage in an estate review, insurance review, retirement review, tax review, and investment review. These financial planners that charge an annual fee usually will use mutual funds to fulfill your investment allocation. The use of mutual funds in this fashion usually results in a two-tiered fee structure, where fees are embedded in the mutual funds and charged by the financial planner on an annual basis. Financial planners that get paid based on what product they use to fulfill your investment strategy will usually sell you "loaded" mutual funds that have a commission (can be as high as 5.25%) up front or sell you an insurance product, such as a variable annuity where the commission paid to the selling broker comes from the insurance company. Financial planners in the sense that I have described in this section, don't really "manage" your money so therefore they should not be charging ongoing fees. But they should be fully compensated upfront for the work that they do.

Pure money managers

Pure money managers can care less about financial planning and focus strictly on returns. Volatility in one's portfolio using this approach typically runs pretty high. Very little customization occurs in these financial arrangements because your money is pooled with other investors and managed only to one mandate. Usually, these "pure" money managers will have multiple strategies to choose from, i.e., large cap value, large cap growth, small cap, etc.

One-stop shop

The one-stop-shop will start with a full assessment of your goals, situation, and overall objectives. Based on these objectives, the advisor will provide advice on broad-based financial planning such as estate planning tips, retirement planning, philanthropic planning tools, and investment allocation. In addition, advisors of the one-stop shop will manage your investment portfolio on an on-going basis. In the case of the one-stop shop or the financial planner arrangement discussed earlier, the advisor does not engage in actual estate planning or tax planning. The role of the advisor is to understand the different tools (see chapter 1) that could be used to help meet your goals and objectives and then work with your attorney and CPA in the implementation of your financial plan. Or, conversely, the advisor can help you implement and understand your estate, tax, gifting, and asset protection strategy once it has been devised by your attorney or CPA. Having somebody that understands your situation and carry through your intended financial strategy when you die is a big benefit to working with an advisor.

Family office

The family office arrangement is the most elaborate of the advisor-client relationships available. This arrangement is a one-stop shop on steroids. Typically, advisors in the family office segment have staff that will negotiate your real estate transactions on your behalf, charter a jet for your family vacation, provide on-staff attorneys to handle your estate and legal matters, manage your investments, provide safe-keeping of your legal documents, and even take your clothes to the dry cleaners. Typically family office relationships are designated for families that have assets in excess of $50 million.

Investment products

Once you have settled on the type of relationship that is suitable for you, the next decision that you and your advisor need to make is what investments to buy. Since a large portion of your overall costs are determined by the products you choose, it is worthwhile to explore these options.

- Individual stocks
  - A portfolio of individual stocks allows you to better control tax consequences because you can decide when you want to sell and when you want to harvest losses. In addition, you have the

flexibility in choosing what stocks you would like to own, which can be a fun thing to do. But management of individual stocks does require more time and attention and usually results in more portfolio volatility than owning a comparable stock mutual fund. Fees associated with managing individual stocks are typically lower than that of a comparable stock mutual fund because managing individual stocks results in only one layer of fees whereas mutual funds have two layers of fees—the internal expense ratio of the fund and the fee paid to the advisor.

- Individual bonds
  - A portfolio of individual bonds gives you the peace of mind that you know what amount you are going to get back and when you will get it. You will get the face value back upon the bond's maturity assuming the issuer does not default. The risk, however, occurs if one of your individual bonds does default; it will have a bigger impact than if you had owned a bond mutual fund, which is typically more diversified. Owning individual bonds is not necessarily cheaper than owning a bond fund because institutions such as mutual funds will buy their bonds in bulk and therefore achieve pricing advantages. Individual bond buyers will usually buy a bond that has already been "marked" up.
- Stock mutual funds
  - Actively managed stock funds will cost you more to implement relative to

individual stocks or indexes. The benefit, however, is they are actively managed by the underlying portfolio manager so you know there is somebody watching the individual stocks within the fund. Individual stock funds are judged by how they do relative to their respective index. For example, a large cap value fund manager will be judged by well how they do against their large cap value index. Stock funds, like all actively managed funds, will distribute capital gains to you. Since you do not manage the stocks in the fund, you cannot control when these gains are distributed, but you have to pay taxes on their distributions.

- Bond mutual funds
  - Actively managed bond funds have the same advantages and disadvantages as actively managed stock funds with the only difference being the investments that underlie the fund. Relative to owning an individual basket of individual bonds, bond funds are more liquid meaning they can be converted to cash more easily than selling an individual bond. Selling your individual bond will largely depend on the price a buyer is willing to pay for the size bond you are looking to sell.
- Indexes
  - Indexes are pre-packaged investments that mimic certain asset classes and sectors of the market. Indexes are not actively managed. Because they are not actively

managed, the fees are low. Indexes provide investors a cheap and diversified method of obtaining exposure to whatever market they want to be exposed to. Many actively managed mutual funds and separate account managers (to be discussed later) are judged relative to their indexes. To justify their fees, mutual funds and separate account managers need to consistently prove their ability to beat their indexes.

- Bond or stock exchange traded funds (ETFs)
    - ETFs are baskets of securities that generally track a chosen index. The benefit of owning an ETF over an index fund is the ability to sell the ETF intraday, whereas open ended mutual funds can only be bought and sold at the close of the day. The fees for ETFs are usually about as low as the embedded fees associated with index open ended mutual funds.
- Separate account managers
    - A separate account manager provides you the benefit of owning individual stocks and having professional management for the portion of your financial portfolio designated to that particular manager. Logistically, a separate account is opened in your name and the separate account manager will buy and sell securities within that account. A separate account manager is similar to a mutual fund in the sense that you achieve professional management for a portion of your portfolio, but you also enjoy the benefits of owning the individual

stocks. One benefit of owning the individual stocks is that you can instruct the manager to harvest losses at any time, assuming there are losses to take. With a mutual fund, as you know, you do not own the individual stocks within the fund. Therefore, you can't harvest losses. With a separately managed account investors usually get many trade confirmations because a confirmation has to be generated for every trade that is done in the account. In addition, an account statement can consist of hundreds of pages depending on how many separate account managers you have hired. This can be a nightmare for one's CPA. Separate account managers are judged by how well they do relative to their index. Tracking error occurs when a manager strays too far from their index without a commensurate return to justify this difference. Because of this separate account managers and actively managed mutual funds typically have a tendency to stay close to their index to keep tracking error low. The product costs are similar to mutual funds. Separate account managers carry higher minimums and are considered to be more of an exclusive product offering; however, with the proliferation of these separate account managers, much of the exclusivity has been lost.

- Alternative investments
  - Alternative investments consist of non-traditional asset classes that seek to be

uncorrelated to traditional stock market and interest rate risk. Alternative investments have become popular vehicles for investors since the beginning of the twenty-first century due to the extreme volatility that began with the Tech Wreck in 2000. Alternative investments are also known as absolute return funds because their goal is to achieve positive returns regardless of market conditions—including declining markets. Hedge and private equity funds are examples of alternatives investments. While many of the early hedge funds took large bets and were therefore were very risky, many of them now have a firm mandate toward risk management. Many of these early alternative investments were formed as limited liability companies (LLCs) so they were illiquid and required significant minimum investments. Because alternative investments are now making their way into mainstream investment strategies in order to deal with the market volatility that has not been seen since the Great Depression, they are now being offered in the traditional mutual fund format so they are more easily accessible. Since a great deal of manager skill and sophistication is involved with many absolute return strategies, caution should be heeded in determining the extent of exposure in one's portfolio. However, the benefit of alternative investments is unquestionable as investment returns need to be generated somehow. The product fees associated with alternative strategies are typically higher than traditional asset class actively managed mutual funds. Some examples of alternative strategies include:

- Global macro funds – funds that make bets depending on the direction of global trends where exit and entry points are important considerations.
- Arbitrage funds – funds that seek to exploit mispricing between similar securities.
- Event driven funds – funds that seek to benefit from anticipated events such as merger and acquisition, settlement of pending lawsuits, management changes, or other key announcements.
- Long/Short funds – funds that buy stocks that have a catalyst for upside returns and shorts stocks that have a catalyst for downside returns. Shorting stocks is a strategy that benefits when stock values are dropping.
- Momentum funds – funds that increase in value when the market is exhibiting a strong trend, either up or down.
- Fund of funds – a fund that invests in a multitude of alternative strategies.

Tactical investment strategies

Tactical investing is the process of active management that involves identifying mispriced asset classes or sectors and investing accordingly. This includes "over-weighting" asset classes that will go up relative to the other asset classes or "under-weighting" asset classes that will go down relative to other asset classes. It is this area of tactical investment strategies that differentiates the multitude of people in the industry. Helping people have success in tactical investing is important because this is how the industry justifies charging fees every year. I do not want to minimize the broader financial planning that firms in the industry offer. It is very important to perform the adequate planning of your estate, retirement, philanthropic endeavors, and gifting strategies, but these planning items do not need to be performed every year. Updating your broader financial strategy is really something that needs to be done every three to five years. It is hard to justify paying annual fees for a process that only takes place once every three to five years. Some firms don't believe that tactical investing can add any value at all and advocate a buy and hold index strategy. In this case, you can't justify charging any fees.

As I've illustrated here, hiring an advisor is not the easiest decision to make. You have to determine what structure fits best with you. Are you looking for a one-stop shop, a pure money manager, a financial planner only, a fee-based structure, or a commission-based structure? Moreover, you have to make sure that the advisor's choice of investment products take into consideration your preferences and is cost efficient. But no matter how daunting this process may be, educating yourself is worthwhile because it can mean the difference between financial success or failure and financial peace of mind or a life of financial anxiety.

Question and answer:

Question: You have covered a lot, just cut to the chase and tell me what advisor-client relationship and mix of investment products you feel is best.

Answer: Only you can decide what type of relationship you want. Everybody is different. However, when it comes to choosing the investment products that will ultimately fulfill your investment strategy, I err on the side of having lower cost products than higher cost products. In addition, I am always in favor of investments that can add to the overall diversification and returns of one's investment portfolio. I find that an efficient product mix that balances cost, practicality, and effectiveness consists of individual stocks, stock index ETFs, individual bonds, bond index ETFs, selective use of actively managed mutual funds or separately managed accounts, and a broad array of alternative investments. In general, I think alternative investments should comprise between 8 percent and 26 percent of a portfolio depending on the risk level and objective.

Hiring a good financial advisor, money manager, financial planner, broker, portfolio manager, or whatever else you want to call them is very important. The four most important things when hiring any professional advisor whether it be a financial person, doctor, or lawyer that you are going to see on a regular basis are trust, service, expertise, and likability. Trust for the obvious reason. Without trust, nothing else matters. Service matters because no matter how talented the advisor is, if they do not have time for you then there is no point to working with them. Expertise is important because at the end of the day you hire somebody to achieve results and knowledge that you can't or don't have the time to achieve on your own. Don't underestimate the idea of likeability. If you can't stand going into your professional advisor's office or you cringe every time you see their name appear on your phone when it rings, then you need to find a different advisor.

If you have interviewed dozens of advisors and none of them exhibit all four of the of the necessary traits—trust, service, expertise, and likeability— try not to get discouraged, there are many advisors out there that rank high in all four areas. Begin by asking for referrals from like-minded people.

Chapter 22

CONCLUSION, IT'S NOT ALL ABOUT MONEY

Jim

I would like to end this book with a story. While I was a portfolio manager for one of the large brokerage firms, I was fortunate to have a client named Jim. Jim was an executive for a large Fortune 500 company. Jim and I became friends. We met every few months to discuss his account, his company, his frustrations, the market, and other changes going on in his life. Ever since I knew him he was planning to retire but always found a reason to stay at his company for "one more project." This went on for years. I left this brokerage firm in January of 2008, but Jim and I had always stayed in touch. We would meet for breakfast and lunch to catch up, talk about the market, and his future plans. I enjoyed meeting with Jim because his insights about leadership, understanding about people, and his unparalleled knack for corporate strategy were all things I aspired to know more about. These meetings gave me a chance to pick his brain. I would ask him how to deal with certain situations I was trying to work through and he would ask me market and other related financial questions. Although Jim traveled all over the country for his job and was one of the busiest executives at his company, he always made time to meet with me, even after I left the brokerage firm where we had met.

One day in November of 2011, Jim was diagnosed with a rare form of cancer. He was to have surgery immediately. It was December before he was well enough to meet. When I spoke with Jim on the telephone that Friday afternoon in December, I sensed in his voice a calm but scared tone. His family was driving in from California and Colorado that day. I quickly left the office, picked up some Vietnamese fried rice, and brought it to his house.

Jim and I talked for a couple of hours, shared tears, and in typical Jim fashion, he enlightened me with advice that could only come from a tried and true leader. He told me how touched he was when a young man he used to mentor who was now head of a division at the company took the time to tell him how important he was in his career and in his life. Jim, with tears in his eyes, told me how much that meant to him. Jim succumbed to his cancer two months later.

Before Jim died, he told me two things that I will never forget:

- Don't ever be afraid to tell people who have had a positive impact in your life your appreciation of the influence they have had. In critical times, these words run deep.
- *"Thoughts create words, words create action, action creates character, and character is everything." –Jim*

While investing has many facets, the cornerstone of the entire process is people and the relationships and human emotions that are shared. No quantity of money in the world can replace the joy brought about in knowing that there are people you trust, love, and respect and that they trust, love, and respect you.

When I asked Jim what he felt was his biggest concern, he told me to make sure my family was taken care of. You'd be amazed by how putting money in its proper perspective can make you a much better investor. *In the end, Jim taught me money should only be a means and never an end in itself.*

Rest in peace, Jim.

Endnotes

1   Bremmer, Ian. "On The Economy, Be Careful What You Wish For". *Foreign Policy* July/August 2011: pp. 60

2   Mauldin, John. "Your Three Investing Options." *John Mauldin.com.* Farenheit Studio, Dec. 24, 2011. Web. Accessed January 2, 2012. http://www.johnmauldin.com /frontlinethoughts/your-three-investing-opponents/

3   Mauldin, John. "Your Three Investing Options." *JohnMauldin.com.* Farenheit Studio, Dec. 24, 2011. Web. January 2, 2012. http://www.johnmauldin.com/ frontlinethoughts/your-three-investing-opponents/

4   Singleton J. Christopher, "Industry Employment and the 1990-91 Recession" 116, *Monthly Labor Review*, (1993), *http://www.questia.com/googleScholar.qst;jsessionid=KPOXCj lvtjYxOLQxWY5gjC9yX5KbbXxkRLvrgY8ZlLJJ5xy3b1pR*

5   Lind Goran, Stefan Ingves, "Stockholm Solutions: A Crucial Lesson from the Nordic Experience is the Need for Prominent State Involvement in Crisis Resolution." *Finance and Development.* Dec 08: 21

6   Amadeo Kimberly, "What is the History of the Gold Standard," article updated Dec. 16, 2011, About.com, A New York Times company, http://useconomy.about.com/ od/monetarypolicy/p/gold_history.htm

[7] John Waggoner, "Should we return to the gold standard," *USA Today*, April 24, 2012.

[8] Chris Martenson uses the phrase "loan into existence" to describe the process of money creation·

[9] Martensen, Chris, "Crash Course: The Next Twenty Years Are Going To Be Completely Unlike The Last," Chapter 8, 2008

[10] Thayers, Watkins, "The Worst Episode of Hyper Inflation in History: Yugoslavia 1993 – 1994," no date of article, The Roger Sherman Society, accessed January 5, 2012, http://www.rogershermansociety.org/yugoslavia.htm

[11] Velocity of Money," Businessdictionary.com, site operated by Webfinance.com, access date January 5th, 2012, http://www.businessdictionary.com/definition/velocity-of-money.html

[12] Bourne, Randolph. "War is the Health of the State" (unpublished essay, 1918), http://struggle.ws/hist_texts/warhealthstate1918.html

[13] Warsh, David, "The Third Coast" (1988-09-04), Boston Globe

[14] Ludwig von Mises, *The Ultimate Foundation of Economic Science: An Essay on Method.* D. Van Nostrand Co, Inc.; Princeton; 1962; pp. 45

[15] Backus, David K., Thomas F. Cooley. "Clear thinking about economic policy," (2011-11-09), *(http://voxeu.org/index.php?q=node/7244)*4

[16] Warsh, David (1988-09-04), "The Third Coast" *(http://www.encyclopedia.com/doc/1p2-8077621.html)*, *The Boston*

Globe, *http://www.encylopedia.com/doc/1p2-8077621.html*, retrieved 2009-11-27

[17] European Central Bank. *Occasional Paper Series* ; No 110; May 2010

[18] "The retreat from everywhere: Led by European banks, the world's lenders are pulling back to their home markets," *The Economist,* April 21, 2012, www.economist.com/node/21553015/print

[19] Paul Kennedy; Fontana Press; 1989....need to locate source and site it properly

[20] Fong, Vanessa (2004). *Only Hope: Coming of Age under China's One-Child Policy.* Stanford, CA: Stanford University Press. pp. 17

[21] Article by Helen Wang; Financial Post; *The biggest story of our time; the rise of China's middle class,* December 24, 2011

[22] Stovall, Sam. "S&P's Guide to Sector Rotation." *Stockcharts. com.* Accessed March 4th 2012, http://stockcharts.com/freecharts/perf.html?[SECT]

[23] http://www.asymmetricinvestmentreturns.com/resource-center/investor-sentiment/using-investor-sentiment-as-a-contrarian-indicato.html

Bibliography

Aliber, Robert. *The New International Money Game.* 6th ed. Chicago: University of Chicago Press, 2002.

Bernstein, Peter. *A Primer on Money, Banking, and Credit.* Hoboken: John Wiley and Sons, 2008.

Blyth, Mark. *Great Transformations:Economic Ideas and Institutional Change in the Twentieth Century.* Cambridge: Cambridge University Press, 2002.

Bonner, Bill, and Addison Wiggin *Empire of Debt: The Rise of an Epic Financial Crisis.* Hoboken: John Wiley & Sons, 2006.

Cohen, J. Benjamin. *International Political Economy: An Intellectual History.* Princeton: Princeton University Press, 2008.

Evensky, Harold, and Deena Katz. *Retirement Income Designed: Master Plans for Distribution: An Advisor's Guide for Funding Boomers' Best Years.* New York City: Bloomberg Press, 2006

Friedman, Milton. *Essays in Positive Economics.* Chicago: The University of Chicago Press, 1953.

Gilpin, Robert. *War and Change in World Politics.* Cambridge: Cambridge University Press, 1981

Gilpin, Robert. *Global Political Economy: Understanding The International Economic Order.* Princeton: Princeton University Press, 2001.

Hazlitt, Henry. *Economics in One Lesson: The Shortest and Surest Way to Understand Basic Economics.* New York: Three Rivers Press, 1979.

Hirsch, Jeffrey and Yale Hirsch. *The Stock Trader's Almanac.* Hoboken: Wiley and Son's, 2012.

Hirsch, Jeffrey and Yale Hirsch. *The Stock Trader's Almanac.* Hoboken: Wiley and Son's, 2008.

Kawasaki, Guy. *The Art of the Star: The Time-Tested, Battle – Hardened Guide for Anyone Starting* Anything. London: Penguin Company, 2004

Lo, Andrew. March/April 2012. "Adaptive Markets and the New World Order." *Financial Analysts Journal* 68(2):18-29.

Maddison, A. *The World Economy: A Millennial Perspective.* Paris: OECD, 2001.

Mises, Von Ludwig. *Human Action: A Treatise on Economics.* 4th ed. San Francisco: Fox and Wilkes, 1963.

Murply, J. John. *Technical Analysis of the Financial Markets: A Comprehensive Guide To Trading Methods and Applications.* Paramus: New York Institute of Finance; 1999

Murphy, J. John. *Intermarket Analysis: Profiting From Global Market Relationships.* Hoboken: John Wiley & Sons, 2004.

Nison, Steve. *Japanese Candlestick Charting Techniques: A Contemporary Guide to the Ancient Investment Techniques of the Far East.* 2nd ed. New York: New York Institute of Finance, 2001.

Pomeranz, K. *The Great Divergence: China, Europe, and the Making of Modern World Economy.* Princeton: Princeton University Press, 2001.

Pompian, Michael. *Behavioral Finance and Wealth Management: How to Build Optimal Portfolios That Account for Investor Biases.* Hoboken: Wiley & Sons, Inc, 2006

Prechter, Robert. *Conquer the Crash: You Can Survive and Prosper in a Deflationary Depression.* Hoboken: Wiley & Sons, 2002.

Prechter, Robert and A.J, Frost. *Elliott Wave Principle: Key to Market Behavior.* 10th ed. Gainesville: New Classics Library, 2005

Pring, Martin. *Investment Psychology Explained*, Wiley & Sons, Inc: New York City, 1993

Rothbard, Murray. *A History of Banking in the United State: The Colonial Era to World War II*. Auburn: Ludwig Von Mises Institute, 2005.

Salerno, Joseph. Introduction to *A History of Money and Banking in The United States*. By Murray N. Rothbard, 7 – 45. Auburn: Ludwig Von Mises Institute, 2005.

Smick, David. *The World is Curved: Hidden Dangers to the Global Economy*. New York City: Penguin, 2008.

Smil, Vaclav. *Global Catastrophe's and Trends: The Next Fifty Years*. Cambridge: The MIT Press, 2008.

Sperandeo, Victor. *Methods of a Wall Street Master*. New York City: John Wiley & Sons, 1993.

Schwartz, Tony. *Be Excellent at Anything: The Four Keys To Transforming The Way We Work And Live*. New York: Free Press, 2010.

Tsoulfidis, Lefteris. *Competing Schools of Economic Thought*. New York: Springer, 2010.